No Surrender!

OTHER BOOKS BY TONY GRAY

Fiction
Starting from Tomorrow
The Real Professionals
Gone the Time
Interlude (*from an original screenplay
        by Lee Langley and Hugh Leonard*)
The Last Laugh

Non-Fiction
The Irish Answer
The Record Breakers (*with Leo Villa*)
Psalms and Slaughter
The Orange Order
Buller (*with Henry Ward*)

TONY GRAY

No Surrender!

THE SIEGE OF
LONDONDERRY 1689

MACDONALD AND JANE'S · LONDON

© Tony Gray 1975
First Published in Great Britain in 1975 by
Macdonald and Jane's
(Macdonald & Co. (Publishers) Ltd.)
Paulton House,
8 Shepherdess Walk,
City Road,
London N1
Printed and bound in Great Britain by
REDWOOD BURN LIMITED
Trowbridge and Esher
ISBN 0 356 08134 6

Contents

List of Illustrations

Acknowledgments

First I should like to thank Dr Patrick Henchy, Director of the National Library of Ireland, and his staff who were extremely helpful in guiding me through a mass of material, printed and manuscript, on the subject of Londonderry and its siege and who also provided me with some of the illustrations. I should also like to thank Dr J.G. Simms, lecturer in history at Trinity College, Dublin, and author of books both on the siege of Londonderry and on the Jacobite Wars in Ireland, who not only gave me a good deal of his time to discuss aspects of the siege which puzzled me, but also lent me some rare, old books on the subject and finally went through the proofs and put me right on a number of points I had missed; if I have not always incorporated changes he suggested, for valid reasons of my own, he must not bear any blame for conclusions I have drawn from events. I am also extremely grateful to my friend Brian Lewis who was good enough to go through the typescript and give me his expert advice on military matters in the seventeenth century. Lastly, I should like to thank Patrick Annesley, then the editor at Macdonald and Jane's, who first suggested the idea of writing the book, and Richard Johnson, who succeeded him.

Ireland at the time of the siege

Introduction

'Whole towns, the seats of the Protestant population, were left in ruins without an inhabitant. The people of Omagh destroyed their own dwellings so utterly that no roof was left to shelter the enemy from the rain and wind. The people of Cavan migrated in one body to Enniskillen. The day was wet and stormy. The road was deep in mire. It was a piteous sight to see, mingled with the armed men, the women and children weeping, famished and toiling through the mud up to their knees. All Lisburn fled to Antrim; and, as the foes drew nearer, all Lisburn and Antrim came pouring into Londonderry. Thirty thousand Protestants, of both sexes and every age, were crowded behind the bulwarks of the City of Refuge. There, at length, on the verge of the ocean, hunted to the last asylum, and baited into a mood in which men may be destroyed, but will not easily be subjugated, the imperial race turned desperately to bay.'

Thus Macaulay in Volume IV of his history of England sets the scene for the greatest siege in the history of these islands — a siege which still holds a sacred place in the race memory of the Ulster Protestant and is yearly celebrated by a march around the walls of the city by the 'descendants' of the Apprentice Boys who shut the gates in the face of King James's Catholic army in 1689.

After 102 days, three ships smashed a boom which had been erected across the river to prevent succour from reaching the beleaguered city by sea. One of these ships, the *Mountjoy*, was commanded by Captain Micaiah Browning, a native of Londonderry, who was killed as his vessel ran the gauntlet of the Irish cannons, and died, as Macaulay puts it, 'by the most enviable of all deaths, in sight of the city which was his birthplace, which was his home, and which had just been saved by his courage and self-devotion from the most frightful form of destruction.'

By then the garrison had been reduced from about seven thousand fighting men to less than three thousand, and the swollen civilian population had become a horde of diseased, hollow-eyed, starving skeletons, kept alive by the intensity of their faith and by their determination to preserve their city forever for the Protestant succession.

That, at least, is the legend: that it was a siege won not by the skill of the soldiers nor by the science of the engineers, but by the sheer tenacity and courage of a population which preferred to live on cats, vermin and carrion rather than submit to a Catholic King and his powerful mixed army of French and Irish Papists.

To quote Macaulay again: 'Five generations have since passed away; and still the wall of Londonderry is to the Protestants of Ulster what the Trophy of Marathon was to the Greeks . . . the whole city is to this day a monument of the great deliverance.'

Three further generations have passed away since Macaulay wrote those words and the tenacity of the Ulster Protestants has not diminished one whit. Bewildered by the support which the first, tentative, civil rights demonstrations in Londonderry received from their 'own' people across the water, and in the 'imperial' press; besieged, as they believed, both by the enemy without and the enemy within; and betrayed, it seemed, even by their own beloved monarchy, for which they imagined they had suffered so much and would be prepared to suffer as much again, the Protestants of Ulster turned to their bibles and their history books knowing in their hearts that they have always had, and always will have, God on their side, whatever may occur in their unhappy province. For them Londonderry has always been the ultimate symbol of defiance, the rock that withstood the onslaught of an overwhelming and evil force, and so saved one small corner of the Kingdom for the Protestant faith forever.

And yet the facts are very different. According to Jacobite accounts of the affair, the inhabitants of Londonderry were so much better armed and equipped, relatively speaking, and so much more comfortably housed than their assailants, that the mystery is that they did not sally out far more often and wreak far greater vengeance on their ailing, ill-equipped and almost defenceless besiegers. The siege of Londonderry was, in any event, quite unnecessary; if, instead of wasting his time and his manpower in trying to reduce it, James had taken a substantial force of Irish soldiers and crossed straight to Scotland, he might there have assembled around him an army formidable enough to challenge William of Orange before the Dutch prince had established a firm foothold in England. If this had happened, Londonderry, bereft of any chance of supplies from England, would have had to come to terms with the Irish administration, and the siege, so far from occupying the prime place it has always held in the annals of Ulster, might have been long since forgotten.

But King James decided obstinately that Londonderry must be reduced before he proceeded with his plans for the recapture of his former kingdom, and went about it so ineptly, and wasted so much time over it, that in the end it could be said to have cost him his kingdom and to have assured the Protestant succession in the British Isles at least until our own times.

It is perhaps not surprising that almost all of the existing accounts of the siege have been written from the point of view of the besieged. After all, a successful stand for 105 days against what they still believe was a massive Catholic professional army, with no help from across the water, is something more to crow about than a dismal and, in the end, unsuccessful attempt to besiege a stubborn city.

There is no new material as such in this book; indeed, it is doubtful if any material still exists to be unearthed about an event which occurred so long ago in such a remote part of the Kingdom, at a time when documentation was sketchy and often as inaccurate as it was incomplete. I have gone back in many cases to the original source material but I found it so intelligently and so remorselessly milked by earlier writers on this subject that there was clearly nothing to be gained from pursuing this course. Instead, what I have tried to do is extract, from all the existing accounts of the siege, a clear, straightforward and, I hope, objective account of the events in Ireland during the winter of 1688 and the spring and summer of 1689*, and a brief run-down on the circumstances which led up to the siege of Londonderry, putting things in what seems to me their proper perspective.

It is important to take a new and objective look at the siege of Londonderry at the present time for, throughout the troubles which have agonized the province of Ulster since 1968, Londonderry and its unassailable walls have remained a powerful element in the Protestant mythology which has helped to keep alive that spirit of fierce intransigence seen at its most virulent, perhaps, in the outpourings of the Rev. Dr Ian Paisley. Countless writers about Northern Ireland have referred to what they describe as the 'siege mentality' of the Ulster Protestant – and that mentality stems chiefly from the siege of Londonderry.

The Ulster Protestants today think of the border which now cuts them off from their neighbours in the Republic as a wall, just like the Londonderry wall, which must be defended with the same courage and vigilance both from the enemy without and from the enemy within. And in Ireland, where so many people still live in the past, and so many myths still remain to be exploded, it is important to take a clear, cold look at what actually did happen in and around

---

*Apparent inconsistencies in dates of events in this period are due to two factors. Until 1752, England used the Julian or Old Style calendar which, after 1700, was eleven days behind the New Style Gregorian calendar used on the Continent. Thus, although the Battle of the Boyne took place on 1 July, it is today celebrated on 12 July. There is a further complication in the fact that whereas on the Continent the new year began, as it does in Britain now, on January 1, in England it began on Lady Day, 25 March. 25 March 1689 would have been followed by 26 March 1690; thus William and Mary were proclaimed King and Queen in February 1688 according to the English reckoning of the period, but in February 1689 according to the Continental New Style reckoning in use everywhere today. To complicate matters still further, Ireland used the Old Style but while Scotland used the Old Style in relation to dates, it used the New Style in reckoning the start of the new year. To avoid confusion when quoting from contemporary documents, etc, I have used the Old Style when referring to dates but have taken the year as starting on 1 January.

Londonderry during those legendary days.

In military terms the whole thing was a total shambles. A weak, arrogant, vacillating Catholic English King sent an ill-trained, ill-equipped, badly-officered army of raw Catholic Irish recruits to lay siege to an over-crowded, inadequately-fortified walled city in which some 30,000 Protestant refugees — including some 7,000 amateur and professional soldiers — were crowded. At no time were the inmates of Londonderry unanimously decided among themselves whether to fight on or surrender — the monolithic solidity of the garrison is another myth — and at times the garrison was led by men as vacillating and inept as King James, some of them possibly indeed 'traitors' to the Protestant cause, but equally possibly merely misguided men who could not bring themselves to believe that the puny garrison would be able to hold out for long against a King and an army led by French commanders of considerable experience. The defence of the city was at times as muddled and mishandled as its investment by these French generals who were utterly baffled by the Irish climate and character and totally defeated by the lack of equipment for a siege and the absence of any military personnel with the skill or knowledge to use what there was effectively. The attempts made by King William's Protestant forces to relieve the city were, perhaps, in the circumstances, even more inept and vacillating, and although it is true that in the end three ships did break the boom and get through to the city, they could just as easily have done so — saving in the process a great deal of terrible and unnecessary suffering — six weeks earlier.

After the initial enthusiasm of the 'mob' had burnt itself out, a small group of fanatically determined Protestant clergymen, amateur soldiers and burghers used every possible means, including censorship (in the sense that they tried to keep the news of what was really happening from the inhabitants as a whole) and the threat of imprisonment and death, to intimidate the garrison and citizens; in the Ulster expression, they 'saw to it' that there would be no talk of surrender, whatever the people might feel about it. Again, one can see parallels here behind Northern Ireland's border today. And they were successful; by one means or another, they managed to persuade the people of Londonderry to hold out until at long last the relief force sent by King William summoned up the necessary courage or decisiveness to attempt to smash the boom.

But the garrison did hold out: this fact alone has emerged from the mists of time and has encouraged generations of Ulster Protestants to think of themselves as the natural heirs and successors to the heroic defenders of Londonderry – and I am not denying that there were moments of almost farcical heroism coupled with an almost equally insane fortitude during the siege – and to develop in them the kind of blank intransigence which has made world opinion despair of ever finding an answer to the Irish Question.

It is, however, equally important that all the other facts surrounding the siege of Londonderry should be known and seen in a fresh perspective: hence this book.

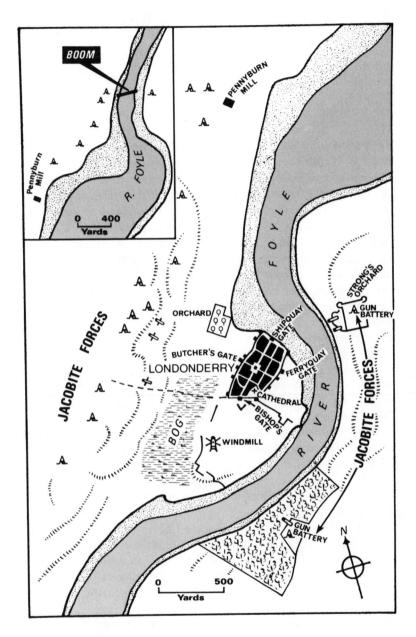

The town of Londonderry

I   *How Derry became Londonderry*

To understand the presence in Londonderry of that staunch band of Protestant diehards of English and Scottish descent determined to hold the fortress at all costs for the Protestant Ascendancy, it is necessary to skim back through the pages of history. English readers are often puzzled and irritated by this Irish tendency to hark back to what happened in history; but to understand any Irish question it is absolutely necessary to go right back to the beginnings because one is dealing with a people who are prisoners of their own past. As the old saying has it: 'The English never remember; the Irish never forget.' There are people in Ireland who would say that since a great many of the almost insoluble minority problems throughout the world in recent years have come about as the direct result of the British policy of colonization in former times, perhaps the English have good reason not to want to remember; most people in England would reply that they cannot be held responsible for things that happened 300 or 700 years ago.

Both points of view have some validity, but the fact remains that it is impossible to fathom what is happening in Ireland at any given time without going back over the centuries. I have done it before, in earlier books, and readers of these must bear with me if I appear to be retracing my footsteps.

The early rulers of Ireland were Gaelic Celts, a fair-haired race of men who came to Ireland from somewhere around the source of the Danube about 350 BC and who with their iron weapons had easily defeated the bronze-armed earlier inhabitants of the island, who had come from Spain.

The Celts were in the habit of making forays on Britain and Normandy and according to legend returned from one of these expeditions with a prisoner they had captured from a

Christian settlement in Wales — a young boy called Patrick. He was a Roman citizen, but the Romans were by now withdrawing from the far-flung outposts of their empire and could do nothing to save young Patrick. He was sold into slavery, and brought up as a shepherd on the slopes of a mountain in Co. Antrim. Eventually he escaped to the continent, studied for the priesthood and returned to Ireland in AD 432 as a bishop, determined to spread Christianity among the savage peasants with whom he had spent his youth. In this endeavour he was signally successful, and Ireland soon became an ecclesiastical centre of Christian learning that was famed throughout the continent.

For some reason, the Romans never crossed that short stretch of water between Holyhead and Dun Laoghaire except as traders. But the Danes came to Ireland, and after them the Normans. A Norman expeditionary force landed at Waterford in 1170 under the command of the Earl of Pembroke, known as Strongbow. He conquered Waterford and was just settling in, preparatory perhaps to breaking away from England and establishing his own independent Norman monarchy in Ireland, when Henry II of England arrived with an army of knights to prevent just this situation and to make sure that Ireland became part of his own personal kingdom. Ignoring the Irish monarchical structure, Henry parcelled up the land of Ireland between various of his Norman barons and the few native provincial kings who agreed to pay annual tributes to Britain. He did this under the authority of a Papal Bull bestowing Ireland upon Britain. The Pope of the period — the first and only British one, Nicholas Brakespeare by name — supported the Anglo-Norman efforts to establish control over Ireland because he had become alarmed at the wide divergence between the monastic Irish Church and mainstream Christianity, and he felt that a strong system of Norman feudal government would be likely to bring the Irish Church back into line.

For a time the Norman conquerors of Ireland had to fight to hold on to the lands they had acquired from the Crown, and they spread their power piecemeal, attempting to reproduce in Ireland the whole feudal pattern of manors and abbeys, castles and fortresses. Eventually their presence came to be accepted by the native Irish, while the Normans, for their part, began to adopt Irish habits and customs and even the Irish language. This was frowned on in England, where the monarchs feared a line-up between the Anglo-Norman barons and the ancient Irish chieftains. The subsequent attempts to extend English law to Ireland resulted in the overthrow of the whole Irish social system, in particular the custom under which the land belonged to the people, who were free to choose their own king or ruler. Under the Norman,system, all the land belonged to the king, and no one could possess land except by grant from him.

The first Parliament of Ireland was convoked towards the end of the thirteenth century. The native Irish were not invited to attend and all business was conducted in French and English. This parliament passed a set of laws which clearly identified the colonists, not as Anglo-Normans living in Ireland, but as English subjects, and they made it illegal for the colonists to intermarry with the Irish, or dress in the Irish style, or recognize the ancient Irish 'Brehon' laws, or speak Gaelic. Thus the settlers were forced into the position of a 'foreign' colony, set among a hostile, 'different' population; they were forbidden, in effect, to assimilate.

It needed only the Reformation to add an element of bitterness to the deep dichotomy which now existed between the native Irish and their overlords. The Reformation never made any headway among the native Irish, partly because the Tudor officials who were sent over to achieve it did not speak Gaelic and the native Irish spoke nothing else, and partly because the monasteries, convents, abbeys and other institutions which might have been used to spread the reformed religion were all suppressed as a result of the Reformation.

The Reformation also added to the Crown's difficulties with the Anglo-Norman colonists, for it had the effect of making many of the settlers, who objected to the new religion, side with the native Irish.

Aware of this, and aware, too, that he could no longer hold the country under an ancient Papal Bull when he had so signally failed to recognize the Pope's authority in other matters, Henry VIII had the title 'King of Ireland' conferred on him by edict of the Irish Parliament in the presence of many of the Irish and Anglo-Norman chieftains and barons. At the same time he tried out a new policy to make the ruling classes in Ireland more dependent upon him. He made the Irish and the Anglo-Norman chieftains and barons surrender their lands to him and receive them back, to be held by knight-service. Thus some of the leading Irish chieftains acquired English titles, which explains how families like the O'Neills of Ulster came to hold such English-sounding titles as the Earls of Tyrone.

When a simple order in the name of the boy king Edward VI made the saying of Mass illegal, it was inevitable that there would be religious clashes in Ireland.

One of the first of these came in 1579 when James Fitzmaurice Fitzgerald, one of the Anglo-Norman nobles of Munster, tried to achieve a Catholic alliance of Irish and Anglo-Irish aristocracy; by now, the Anglo-Normans had come to be known as Anglo-Irish. He went to the continent and drummed up a mixed force of Italians and Spaniards, financed jointly by the Pope and the King of Spain who were both anxious for their own reasons to take a slap at Protestant England. Returning with a small force accompanied by a party of priests who preached rebellion as a sacred duty, he landed at Kerry and entrenched himself in the Dingle peninsula, but his revolt was soon snuffed out by the Lord Deputy of the day, Lord Grey de Wilton.

Still, the episode was significant for two reasons: it was the first of many attempts by the Irish to unseat the English with the aid of forces from continental Europe, and it was followed by savage reprisals which set the pattern for generations to come. After the surrender, the Lord Deputy systematically destroyed all the food in West Munster and managed to achieve a famine of considerable proportions.

As a further reprisal for the rebellion, Queen Elizabeth confiscated vast tracts of Catholic-owned land in the south-west of Ireland and turned it over to English settlers. But although men could be found in plenty to take over nominal ownership of the land, and to charge rent for it, English settlers ready to work the land in this savage and unknown corner of the British Isles were not so easy to find, and the 'undertakers' – as the speculators were called – soon discovered that they could get better results by allowing the Irish to creep back illegally and pay rent for the privilege of farming their own land as tenants.

This policy was not Elizabeth's innovation; the practice of clearing the rebellious Irish off their lands and 'planting' these lands with colonies of loyal English farmers and landlords had already been started during the reign of the Catholic Queen Mary.

It was this policy which was to lead to all the troubles in Ulster.

Ireland, at this time, was divided into a pattern of counties, along much the same lines as the English shires, but superimposed on this was an older pattern which had survived from Celtic times when Ireland was divided into five 'fifths' or provinces. These were the four provinces which still exist – Ulster in the north, Munster in the south, Connaught in the west and Leinster in the east. The fifth province, which had long disappeared, was the small Kingdom of Tara in Co. Meath not far from Dublin, from which these four provinces were originally ruled by a High King.

Until now, Ulster had remained the most Gaelic and the most Catholic part of the country. The next rebellion, which amounted in effect to the last stand of the old Gaelic Catholic aristocracy, came about when two nobles who between them controlled almost all of Ulster – Hugh O'Neill of Tyrone and Hugh O'Donnell of Tyrconnell (the modern Donegal) – rose up against Elizabeth's forces and for nine years waged war on them. Their revolt spread to the other Gaelic chieftains in the country; they imported a force of Spanish troops to assist them, but in the end were defeated by superior arms and organization.

The submission of Hugh O'Neill in 1603 is one of the watersheds in Irish history. Although he was pardoned, and most of his lands were restored to him, things in Ireland were never the same again.

During the O'Neill rebellion, an elaborate system of fortified posts had been established throughout Ulster, and after the rebellion was over the garrisons in these forts were maintained so that O'Neill had the feeling that he was everywhere being supervised by the British military. English law and administration now replaced the old Gaelic system; sheriffs and justices of the peace were appointed and assizes on the English pattern were held. The old Irish system of land tenure disappeared completely to be replaced by the English feudal system.

Perhaps even more important from O'Neill's point of view, the English Protestant Church was established in the area on a firm basis, backed by the English officials. Until now, the Reformation had hardly affected Ulster at all. Religious houses continued to be occupied by monks and friars despite Henry VIII's Act of Dissolution – indeed there were friars in Londonderry when the siege began in 1689 – and even in the city of Armagh, seat of the Primate, and technically the centre of the established Protestant Church of Ireland, there were priests appointed by Rome. O'Neill had always been the champion of the Catholic cause in Ulster and for him the last straw must have been a proclamation made from his own manor at Dungannon, commanding all Jesuits and priests deriving their authority from Rome to quit the kingdom forthwith.

The government officials and military authorities who now effectively ran Ulster resented the fact that O'Neill and the other rebel Gaelic chieftains had been allowed to keep most of their lands, and they made life as difficult as possible for them, constantly accusing them of intriguing with Spain or with the Pope. Life in Ulster in these circumstances soon became very tedious to O'Neill and to O'Donnell's successor – O'Donnell himself had died in exile after the rebellion – and when O'Neill was summoned to London to answer charges which had been made against him, he decided to go into exile in a chartered vessel; and, accompanied by most of Ulster's leading Gaelic chieftains, he left Ireland for ever.

This 'Flight of the Earls' as it was called was held to be treason and opened the way for another plantation, in some ways the most successful of them all: the Plantation of Ulster.

While preparations for the Plantation of Ulster were under way, Sir Cahir O'Doherty, Lord of Inishowen, and one of the Ulster nobles who had not gone abroad with Hugh O'Neill, staged a futile revolt during which he captured the fort of Culmore just outside Derry, and set fire to the town of Derry. There had been a proclamation to the effect that the native inhabitants of Tyrone and Donegal would not be disturbed in their possessions if they behaved themselves, but this revolt of Cahir O'Doherty's gave the administration the excuse they needed to extend the scope of the plantation. It was now decided to replant the whole area of Donegal, Coleraine (today a part of Co. Londonderry), Armagh, Fermanagh, Tyrone and Cavan. The British authorities held very high hopes for this plantation. The land was fertile and, under more advanced methods of cultivation than the Irish had ever dreamed of using, could have vastly increased its output; and the proximity of Scotland and England assured a market for this output. The confiscated land could be used to recompense those who had served the Crown during the O'Neill rebellion — soldiers and civilians alike — and who had not yet been paid for their efforts. With loyal and peaceable Scots and English settlers on the land, in place of the savage and rebellious Celts, the whole area might be transformed into a prosperous and law-abiding province, which would not only provide revenue for the Crown, but even more important, would ensure that the area could never again be used as a base for a rebellion or an attack on England from the continent.

This was a period when colonization was very much in the air — only a few months before the Flight of the Earls, the first party of English colonists had set out for Virginia — and it was then widely thought, ridiculous as it seems today, that it was necessary to find new colonies because London was becoming overcrowded.

To attract planters, rents were low and there were other inducements such as the building of forts, storehouses and bridges. For this reason, the administration felt confident enough to lay down certain conditions. The settlers were to be men of substance and not mere fortune-hunters, and they were to settle in the areas of the greatest danger, along the sea coast and in the interior, where their presence would be of the greatest value to the Crown. They were expected to build castles and fortified houses, erect civilized towns and villages, and to cultivate their land in the English fashion. The Irish stayed on in these towns and villages, as tenants on what had formerly been their own lands, and the swordmen — the armed followers of the Gaelic chieftains who had always maintained their own private armies — were to be transported to the wastelands of Connaught or obliged to join the army. In practice most of these men, who knew no other trade than war, simply took to the woods from which they began to harass the settlers as soon as they arrived.

At a very early stage in the plantation negotiations, overtures were made to the City of London to see whether the City Guilds would be interested in taking over a large block of the confiscated land and developing it as a collective undertaker; the area considered most suitable was the town called Derry and some of the adjoining countryside in Coleraine. There were plenty of precedents for this approach to the City. The City had often in the past come to the assistance of the Crown — it had in fact made a couple of sizeable contributions to the cost of putting down O'Neill's rebellion — and the proposition could be represented in the light of offering the City a favour, while at the same time King James's advisers felt that the City's participation in the scheme would give it the prestige it needed to attract other substantial investors.

Full details of the project were worked out by Sir Thomas Philips, who presented the City with a document setting out what the costs were likely to be and what profits could be expected to accrue; he also provided a prospectus setting out the natural resources and economic potentialities of the area. An official government prospectus followed, stressing the advantages of Coleraine and Derry — particularly the latter which could very easily be rendered impregnable, and was the only sizeable port in the whole of Ulster — and pointing out that the King had agreed to create Corporations in both towns. This prospectus also listed the inducements that were being offered: the benefits of the customs on all exports and imports for twenty-one years. Admiralty rights, rights to the salmon fisheries on the Bann and Foyle rivers, and so on.

After a good deal of discussion, the City decided to invest in the project and sent a deputation to take a look at the area. Four wise, discreet and grave citizens, according to T.W. Moody's very comprehensive survey of the affair, *The Londonderry Plantation, 1609—41*, did a tour of the district with Sir Thomas Philips; and it was a real public relations exercise. Great care, Moody says, was taken to ensure that these distinguished visitors would receive only the best impressions of the countryside. Their conductors were to be experienced and plausible people, able to silence disturbing rumours, to lead their guests along the most attractive paths, concealing from them anything distasteful, and the visitors were to be well fed and comfortably housed, preferably in English houses. What they were shown far exceeded their expectations — Ireland did not enjoy a particularly high reputation in England at this time — and as a final, masterly promotional touch, they were each supplied, at extremely favourable rates, with a selection of samples of some of Ulster's staple produce: raw hides, tallow, salmon, herrings, eels, pipe staves, yarn and iron ore.

Notwithstanding the glowing report the deputation put in on their return, the London companies were not all keen on the project and some had to be fined before they would agree to co-operate. Some of the contributions to the scheme were pitifully small, as little as £1 in a few cases, and many of the companies pleaded that they could not afford to put any money at all into the scheme. Nevertheless it went ahead, and the City of London undertook to develop and defend Derry and the area around it; and to mark the decision, the name of the city was changed to Londonderry.

It might be useful at this point to clear up the question of Derry and Londonderry. Originally the place was called Derry; the word, based on the Gaelic 'dairghe', means oak or oak-wood, and at one time the town's full name was Derry-Calgach, the oak-wood of the fierce warrior. After its take-over by the London livery companies, and indeed ever since, many Catholic Irish have insisted on continuing to refer to it as Derry, omitting the London part, as a gesture of protest. Curiously, the Ulster Protestants don't seem to feel all that strongly about this matter — there are references to Derry's walls in many of the loyalist ballads and some of the contemporary Protestant accounts of the siege constantly refer to Derry, though Ulster politicians are usually careful to stress the *London* in Londonderry. In this book I have stuck to Londonderry both to avoid confusion and because, after the beginning of the seventeenth century, that was the official name of the place — though naturally I have used the word Derry when quoting from people who called it that, and when referring to the city before the London livery companies took it over.

Londonderry is on the western or Donegal side of the Foyle, about five miles from the point where that river enters Lough Foyle. The hill or 'Island' of Londonderry — at one time it was an island — which has been described as a natural acropolis of the North, ascends to an elevation of 119 feet and covers 200 acres, but even as early as the seventeenth century the city had spread westwards towards the Bogside, north along the bank of the river Foyle and along the opposite bank of the Foyle, in the district known as Waterside.

In Celtic times, around the fifth century, the whole area became the property of Owen, the son of the most famous of all the Celtic kings, Niall of the Nine Hostages, which explains why it was known as Inishowen (the island of Owen); today, only the peninsula between Lough Foyle and Lough Swilly retains this name.

In the middle of the sixth century, St Columba established a monastery in Derry and the town became a monastic centre. It was plundered by the Norsemen and burnt down several times before the year 1200, but remained an ecclesiastical centre with churches, a cathedral and religious houses until the sixteenth century.

When the Normans came to Ireland it was of interest as a strategic site and was sacked by John de Courcy and finally granted by Richard II to Richard de Burgh.

It became a strategic point again in the Tudor wars against the native Irish; when Shane O'Neill, then Earl of Tyrone, rebelled against Queen Elizabeth, the then Lord Deputy

Sydney sent Edward Randoll by sea to Derry, to fall on O'Neill's forces from the rear. Randoll defeated O'Neill but his successor was forced to abandon Derry when the powder magazine exploded accidentally in 1588, blowing up the town and the fort, and demolishing some of the ancient monastic buildings which had survived until then.

Derry was then again taken over by the native Irish until, in 1600, another Lord Deputy, Mountjoy, sent Sir Henry Dowcra to recapture Derry and plant a colony there. He converted it into a trading town and obtained a charter for it in 1604.

Then, as we have seen, in May 1608, while the preparations for the Plantation of Derry by the City of London companies was under way, the Irish chieftain Sir Cahir O'Doherty, Lord of Inishowen, attacked Derry, put the garrison to the sword and plundered and burnt the town.

In 1613, Derry became Londonderry and its citizens were, by charter, incorporated under the name of 'The Mayor, Commonality and Citizens'. The Corporation continued, except during the interruptions of the Commonwealth and King James's Irish war, to exercise their powers and to return members of parliament (two to the Irish parliament, and, after the Union, one to Westminster) who were elected by Freemen.

Between 1617 and 1633, the famous walls of Londonderry — there had been earlier, more rudimentary walls — were laid out and built at a cost of over £8,000 which was defrayed by the City of London, and the Market House and Cathedral were built.

During the rebellion of 1641, Londonderry was secured from the rebels by Sir Frederick Hamilton and defended by the Lagganeers — a fierce fighting force of Protestants from the Laggan, that fertile area between the Foyle and Swilly rivers. Preparations were made for a long siege which never came. As in the later siege, the city was defended by soldiers who were principally landholders from the surrounding district; the gates and walls were manned day and night; suspect Catholics were expelled and forbidden to return on pain of death; and houses and orchards were pulled down for the better defence of the city. But although Sir Phelim O'Neill was prowling around the area with a rebel army threatening to clear all the Protestants out of Donegal and Tyrone, Londonderry was never attacked.

In 1648, during the Civil War in England, Sir Charles Coote took over the governorship of Londonderry and held it for the English parliament until the restoration of the monarchy. In March 1649, the city was blockaded for five months by a mixed force of Royalists and Prelatists, joined eventually by Munro with a party of Scottish Highlanders; this earlier siege of Londonderry is often overlooked, being eclipsed by the second and more celebrated one. Munro was appointed Governor of Coleraine and stepped up the pressure on Londonderry, the only stronghold in Ulster which held out against the Royalists. It was during this attack on Londonderry that a fort was built at a bend in the river called the Crook of Inver, at the point where the boom was later erected; it was called Charlesfort in honour of the king.

II   *The legacy of 1641*

The area taken over by the City of London towards the beginning of the seventeenth century was as different from England as the language of its inhabitants was unlike English. There were no cities or towns of any size; Derry, now Londonderry, the principal one, probably had no more than 2,000 inhabitants, if that many, and elsewhere the natives lived mostly in scattered hamlets. Their cabins were squat, oval-shaped, one-roomed structures with walls of clay and wattle and bee-hive thatched roofs not unlike the sort of houses many West African tribesmen live in today. They had neither windows nor chimneys, and the smoke from the fire was hopefully expected to escape through a hole in the roof. By no means all of the native Irish aspired even to so humble a dwelling. Many slept out of doors in all weathers, in the bogs and woods, wrapped in their long, heavy, home-made woollen cloaks. These cloaks, if soaked in water, would keep the wearer warm all night. Not indeed that there was any need, in the Irish climate, to soak them artificially; they were almost permanently damp, a moist cloak during the day and an insulated sleeping bag at night.

They were farmers by trade — cattle ranchers principally, though they carried on a certain amount of tillage, using methods of cultivation which by English standards were extremely crude. There were no enclosed fields, and they used a short plough drawn by five or six horses, attached to it merely by their tails, an inefficient and unscientific system of haulage. Instead of threshing the corn, they burnt the straw away, a method which they considered saved labour — not that there was any shortage of it. They lived mainly on milk, butter, oatmeal and weeds like cress and sorrel. They kept pigs and sometimes ate pork, though many of them ate no meat at all.

While the City of London was drawing up its plans to fortify and develop the area around Londonderry inhabited by these strange, savage Irish peasants, the plantation of the remainder of the confiscated land in Ulster continued apace. Here, as elsewhere in Ireland, it was easy enough to get undertakers to agree to take over and develop the land, but in general they transferred their lands, sold them outright or encouraged the natives to stay on and work the land as tenants. This, of course, undermined one of the principal objectives of the plantation, which had been to get the rebellious Irish natives off their lands, and it also ensured trouble in the future; the tenants were only waiting for the first opportunity to cut their landlords' throats and seize their own lands back. Until such an opportunity arose, they were prepared to go through the motions of pleasing their new masters.

In *The Londonderry Plantation, 1609–41*, Moody puts it this way: 'An utterly insufficient proportion of the escheated land went to the Irish grantees, a grossly excessive proportion to the British undertakers. The plantation scheme required the expulsion of all the native inhabitants from the lands of the latter, and their segregation on those of the former, of the servitors and of the church. The undertakers found it more profitable to retain the natives than to import British colonists, and conspired with the natives to stultify the segregation scheme. A revolt . . . was inevitable. The greater part of the swordmen withdrew to the woods and turned outlaw. These "wood-kernes" became the scourge of the undertakers upon whom they descended when the occasion offered, to plunder and assault.'

In Antrim and Down, where the English and Scots had long held tracts of land, the colonial element was strengthened by further plantations of English and Scots colonists. Elsewhere, almost all the Irish landowners were dispossessed of their farms and the area largely repopulated with Scottish Presbyterians and English Protestants. The plantation which directly followed the Flight of the Earls and the introduction of these new non-Catholic settlers laid the foundations for the partition of Ireland over three hundred years later, and sowed the seeds of the bitter dissension whose effects we have been witnessing over the past six years.

After the Plantation, Ulster was largely in the hands of a people utterly different in race, religion and outlook from the remainder of the Irish nation. In the 'replanted' portion of Ulster, three-quarters of the population were now Protestants — and Protestants with no ties or sympathies whatever with Ireland. Elsewhere, the proportion of Protestants to Catholics was about one to five. But the difference went far deeper than that.

With the Flight of the Earls, most of the ancient Celtic chieftains — many of whom had, as we have seen, accepted English titles and had become the 'gentry' of Ulster — emigrated, with the result that there were now, in effect, no Catholic gentry in Northern Ireland.

Elsewhere in Ireland, many of the old Anglo-Norman feudal overlords had retained the ancient religion, and in times of religious and political strife, often took the Catholic side; indeed, in later years, many of the Irish attempts at rebellion were led and inspired by descendants of the old Norman settlers. Also, the fact that the Protestant gentry in what can loosely be described as southern Ireland were forced, in the nature of things, to meet these Catholic Anglo-Irish gentry who were literally their peers, had the result that the former never adopted the hard-line, anti-Catholic attitude which developed in the North. The Protestant peers in the North were not exposed to Catholic gentry in the same way and consequently tended to think of all Catholics as peasants.

The bulk of the gentry in southern Ireland were, of course, Protestant, and they tended to concentrate in certain areas: in the Pale, that predominantly Protestant and English-orientated area around Dublin; in Cork and Sligo and in odd isolated pockets in the Midlands and dotted all over the countryside, usually, it must be admitted, wherever the land was particularly fertile.

There was yet another difference. Because the Flight of the Earls removed the best of the ancient Celtic blood from the northern province, those Catholic Irish who remained to labour on the farms of the Protestant settlers composed, for the most part, a caste of people which does not tend to produce natural leaders. In southern Ireland, on the other hand, despite all the years of emigration and confiscation, there remained a large number of energetic and enterprising descendants of the ancient Irish families who could meet the Catholic Anglo-Irish gentry on equal terms.

In England, King James I had been succeeded in 1625 by the ill-starred Charles I, who had inherited his father's belief in Divine Right and his hatred of the Puritans. His protracted quarrels with Parliament need not concern us here, but it is important that he called an informal assembly in Ireland, to which he promised certain 'graces'. One of these guaranteed a greater measure of toleration to Catholics; another pledged that the Crown would not claim lands which had been held without challenge for sixty years. In return for these promises, substantial subsidies were paid, but the graces were never granted and Strafford was made Lord Deputy of Ireland.

Strafford was a vigorous ruler, and he succeeded in reducing the country to a greater submission to the Crown than ever before – or since, in fact. He raised a substantial Irish army, which was later his undoing, and he produced a considerable revenue for the Crown. When Charles recalled Strafford, the fact that as Lord Deputy he had raised and trained an army of 8,000 men, in the nature of things largely Catholic, began to create the fear in England and Scotland that he had done so to provide Charles with an army he could use against the Covenanters of Scotland and even the Puritan parliamentarians of England. Consequently the Parliament which Charles summoned in 1640 immediately impeached Strafford, the main charge against him being that he had advised the King to bring over the Irish troops for use in England. His defence was that they were to be used against the Scots only, but the Commons felt that once on British soil they might very well be turned against the forces of Parliament. Charles hesitated as long as possible before giving his assent to the Bill of Attainder, but when rioting mobs began to appear before the palace demanding Strafford's execution, he gave in.

With Strafford gone, the government of Ireland fell to the Lords Justices, Parsons and Borlase, well-meaning men but far too weak to control a country seething with fear and resentment which had been kept in control only by Strafford's firm hand. The landowners and small farmers of Ulster, who had been dispossessed in the plantations, and their descendants, were spoiling for a chance to get their lands back, and the Irish Catholic landowners and farmers elsewhere throughout the country felt — and with very good reason — that if the Puritan element in the British Parliament came out on top, they would bring in further measures against the Catholic religion and seize yet more Irish land for English and Scottish planters.

The King still had Strafford's army to control the situation, but Parliament now argued that it was undesirable to keep such a vast and expensive force in a country which — until that moment — was more peaceful than it had been for centuries, and further that since this army was largely composed of Catholics, it could not be trusted to fight on the Protestant side. The King agreed to a partial demobilization, reducing the total force from Strafford's 8,000 to a mere 3,000. The remainder, 5,000 well-trained, well-disciplined native soldiers, were disbanded. Their arms and ammunition were stored in the vaults of Dublin Castle, and although some of the men went abroad to serve as mercenaries, the bulk of them stayed on in Ireland ready, if the occasion arose, to form the nucleus of a rebellious army.

Owen Roe O'Neill, one of the descendants of Hugh O'Neill, Earl of Tyrone — serving with the Spanish army in Flanders — heard rumours of a forthcoming revolt in Ireland and promised to return as soon as firm plans had been prepared.

It was at this juncture that recusancy fines — that is, fines for failing to attend Protestant divine service — were re-introduced in Ireland. When they were enforced in England, Strafford had very wisely allowed their enforcement in Ireland to be shelved indefinitely because he knew that the imposition of these fines would inflame the Catholic Irish unnecessarily.

Various factions in Ireland now began to plan rebellion, which broke out in 1641. This rebellion, which is often dismissed in history books as a simple massacre of the Protestants by hordes of bloodthirsty Irish Catholics, was complicated by a great many issues. By the beginning of the seventeenth century the population of the country had four main strains: the native Irish; the Anglo-Irish or Old English, that is to say, the descendants of the original Anglo-Norman invaders; the New English, who had come over as planters during the reigns of Mary and Elizabeth, plus, of course, the English merchants and traders in the cities and ports and the English administrators, both civilian and military; and the old Scots-Irish of Ulster. There were now, in addition, the new Scottish and English planters in Ulster, a fifth strain. Most of the Old English were inclined to favour the King in his struggle against Parliament, but some, realizing how weak his position was becoming, were prepared to throw in their lot with the Parliamentarians in the hope of getting a better deal. The New English, the Scots-Irish of Ulster and the new Ulster planters were divided in their loyalties, some favouring the King and some the Commons, so that, with a civil war imminent in England, the English in Ireland were deeply divided among themselves. The native Irish of course wanted to break all connections with England altogether; they planned to evict the English from all their holdings in Ireland and take over the government of the country themselves.

The original plan for the rebellion was to capture Dublin Castle, seize the arms which had been stored there after the demobilization of the greater part of Strafford's army, and at the same time stage an uprising of the Catholic gentry and peasants of Ulster who would be overjoyed at the prospect of taking back their old holdings. The remaining provinces, it was hoped, would then follow suit within a few days, and if serious fighting broke out an Irish army could rapidly be formed from the disbanded remnants of Strafford's army and re-armed with the weapons seized from Dublin Castle.

In Dublin the plot leaked out, due to drunken incompetence. The English merchants and settlers around the Pale – that area near Dublin which had remained continuously under English rule – were armed to defend them-

selves and the attack on the Castle was called off at the last
minute.

But nobody told the conspirators of Ulster what had
happened in Dublin and at dawn on 23 October 1641, gangs
of armed Irishmen descended on the homes of the English
and Scots settlers. The evictions were carried out with
terrible cruelty. The weather was bitterly cold. Without
warning, stripped of everything they possessed, often including their clothes, the Ulster colonists were bundled out
into the savage Irish winter.

Much of the subsequent – and some of the
present – Ulster Protestant mistrust and fear of the Catholics
stems from the events of that terrible winter, petrified in
racial memories. It is true that the Irish who descended on
the English and Scottish settlers in Ulster in October 1641,
and at first evicted and later massacred them in thousands,
were all Catholics, but the reason they did so was not because
they were Catholics and the settlers were Protestants; it was
because they wanted their ancient lands back. Nevertheless,
the difference in religion provided convenient and misleading
labels which could always thereafter be used to whip up
violence in the province.

In the killings, neither man, woman nor child was spared,
as D.M.R. Esson points out in his book, *The Curse of
Cromwell*: 'Indeed, the Irish bloodlust went on to destroy
everything English; the farms were burnt, the horses
hamstrung, the cattle slaughtered. The Irish were bent on
obliterating everything English, or that had even a semblance
of being English. Nothing was sacred, nothing was to be
spared. Wooden structures were burnt, stone buildings were
torn down and it was enough that a dog had prowled around
an English midden for it to be killed; sufficient that a hen had
laid eggs for an English table for its neck to be wrung.'

There were, of course, reprisals. The Protestants of Ulster,
once they got their second wind, began to attack the Irish,
driving off their sheep and cattle and killing any people they
fell upon, sometimes with equal cruelty; but the affair has
gone down in history, and above all in the race memory of
the Ulster settlers, as 'The Massacre of the Protestants'.

In England, Charles's struggle with Parliament had reached its height, and with riots in the streets of London, the King had to flee his capital for Hampton Court. Soon he withdrew by easy stages to Newmarket, Nottingham and then York, and did not return to London until his trial and execution. England was now on the brink of a civil war.

In Ireland the massacres continued. The English Parliament raised a few companies and sent them to reinforce the garrisons; it also passed an Act depriving Irish rebels of their lands and selling them to holders of a new debenture issue who had advanced money for the conduct of the war – to be rewarded later, after the rebellion, either with the rebel lands or with the proceeds of their sale. Among the holders of this stock was Oliver Cromwell.

From the Pale, an army of colonists raided the Wicklow mountains, shooting and hanging as many Irish as they could find and seriously depopulating the area; and in Ulster a Scots force under General Munro began to drive the Irish out of Antrim and Down, exterminating them wherever possible as a matter of policy. By the spring of 1642, the English held Dublin, Drogheda, Kinsale, Cork and Youghal, and a few strongholds like Derry and Enniskillen in Northern Ireland. The rebels were in control of most of the rest of the country, which had been reduced to a wilderness in which troops of starving swordmen fought one another for such scraps of food as had not already been destroyed. At least one-sixth of the population of Ireland disappeared that winter and the survivors could think of nothing more constructive to do than to continue the killing. It has been estimated that one in ten of all the Protestant settlers of Ulster was killed in the initial massacre, some suffering dreadful atrocities.

I have dealt at some length with this 'Massacre of the Protestants' because it was largely the fear of a repetition of it which led to the locking of the gates of Londonderry in the face of King James's troops in 1688.

When the civil war broke out in earnest in England, an uneasy confederation of Catholic Royalist Anglo-Irish gentlemen and Irish rebel leaders entered into a protracted series of negotiations with King Charles which were completed only a few days before his trial.

At the time of the outbreak of the rebellion of 1641, the Anglo-Irish Catholic gentry were initially disposed to side with the English settlers. They had not been molested for their religious views in Strafford's time – he did not want to lose their support – and they were happy enough with the administration; but soon they discovered that the English Puritan Parliament regarded all Catholics, Anglo-Irish gentry and peasants alike, as potential rebels. The result of this was that they were forced to throw in their lot with the rebels, and many of them became commanders of the rebel forces.

They also organized what was known as the Confederation of Kilkenny – so called because it met in Kilkenny, the seat of some of Ireland's earlier parliaments – to provide a central government modelled on the Dublin parliament: an assembly of bishops, abbots and the few Catholic peers that were left who, together with a number of county and borough members, would, hopefully, run the country when things had settled down after the rebellion.

But class distinctions in the fragile fabric of Irish society proved its undoing. The native Irish accused the Anglo-Irish gentry of betraying the rebel cause in order to preserve their own political and social ascendancy; the Anglo-Irish gentry replied that so far from acting out of self-interest, they were risking everything by joining the Confederation, while few of the native Irish had anything to lose other than their lives. The Confederation fell apart in 1649 and it was during its brief life that the phrase 'quarrelling like Kilkenny cats' passed into the English language.

Cromwell's ruthless campaign in Ireland was the Puritan Parliament's way of dealing with the Irish Question; it was designed partly to restore order and partly also to punish both the Irish rebels and the Anglo-Irish Royalists for backing the wrong side in the civil war, and it is likely that the ferocity of Cromwell's troops can be explained by the fact that they genuinely believed that they were bringing the sword of vengeance down on the heads of the Catholic wretches responsible for the terrible massacre of the Protestants in 1641, eight years earlier.

When the military campaign was concluded, Puritan England set about the task of squaring the account with the

Irish Catholic rebels. Many different people, with many different problems, were calling for satisfaction. The soldiers wanted the arrears of pay they were owed, either in cash or in land. The English and Scottish settlers who had been bundled off the holdings they had acquired in the Plantation of Ulster wanted those lands back. The English were united in their demands that the dastardly Irish rebels should be taught a lesson; and both old and new settlers were demanding a far greater measure of security in their holdings.

Now it was proposed that the soldiers who had served Parliament, either in England or in Ireland, and who still had arrears of pay owing, should be compensated by further confiscations of land in Ireland. An Act of Settlement was passed which decreed that everyone in Ireland should lose his property wholly or in part, unless he could prove that he had been consistently faithful to the cause of the English Parliament.

'To Hell or Connaught' was the choice offered to the Irish Catholic landowners and small farmers who could not prove their unswerving loyalty to the Parliamentarians, with the result that when Cromwell had done with the country, less than a quarter of all the land in Ireland remained in Irish Catholic hands, and vast numbers of Irish Catholic families were huddled in small settlements of cabins among the boulder-strewn fields of Connemara, as the barren part of Connaught, west of the Shannon river, was called.

Irish hopes of a change of heart when Charles II was restored to the throne in 1660 were quickly dashed. He cared nothing for Ireland and very little for the dispossessed Royalists there; he tried to compromise, but in reality he had far more to fear from the Cromwellian settlers who were in possession of the newly confiscated lands than he had to fear from the dispossessed Catholic gentry who at this juncture were without effective leadership. In religious matters, he went back to Strafford's highly successful system of *de jure* strictness — to keep the Protestants quiet — combined with *de facto* laxity, to avoid trouble with the Catholics.

But his close alliance with the Catholic King Louis XIV of France and his repeated efforts to achieve religious tolerance created a deep fear in England that Popery was about to be reintroduced. There was an almost medieval intensity about the post-Reformation zeal which swept through England at this period. Both the Great Plague and the Great Fire of London were regarded as being in some way part of a Catholic plot. There were rumours that Charles had embraced the Catholic religion. His mother, Henrietta Maria, was known to be a staunch Catholic, and his brother, the Duke of York and next in line for the throne, was by now openly a Catholic. 'Popery', writes Sir Arthur Bryant in his *Protestant Island*, 'was the bug-bear with which seventeenth-century children were brought up by their mothers and nurses: a terror they never outgrew. They had learnt their religion from the crude woodcuts of Protestants burning at the stake in Foxe's *Book of Martyrs* and their history from tales of the Massacre of St Bartholomew, the Gunpowder Plot and the Irish Rebellion of '41. The Great Fire seemed to them but one more page in that bloodstained mythology, a prelude to some gruesome popish plot of assassination, midnight massacre and foreign invasion.'

And if people felt like this in the relatively civilized atmosphere of London, well-policed and orderly, with a predominantly Protestant population, it is not difficult to understand how the Ulster settlers felt surrounded by venomous, dispossessed Catholic peasants, and farmers whose one ambition in life was to get their ancient lands back, and with the woods around them inhabited by unemployed professional swordsmen, spoiling for a fight.

To make matters worse, during this entire period a whole series of pamphlets were published in Britain, purporting to reveal the secrets of various fearsome Popish plots which were being hatched among the Irish, who were to rise in rebellion and massacre yet more Protestants. In 1680, as a result of the publication of one of these pamphlets (see illustration between pages 40 and 41), the House of Lords sent the following message to the Commons:

> Resolved,
> By the Lords Spiritual and Temporal, and in Parliament Assembled, That they do declare that they are fully satisfied that there now is, and for divers years last past there hath

been, a Horrid and Treasonable Plot and Conspiracy contrived and carryed on by those of the Popish Religion in Ireland, for Massacreing the English, and Subverting the Protestant Religion, and the ancient established Government of that Kingdom, to which their Lordships desire the concurrence of this House.

The Commons replied with the following resolution:

Resolved,
That this House doth agree with the Lords in the said Vote with the addition of these words, *That the Duke of York being a Papist, and the expectation of his coming to the Crown hath given the greatest Countenance and Encouragement thereto, as well as to the Horrid Popish Plot* in the Kingdome of England

James II became king in 1685, when his brother died of a stroke at the age of fifty-five. A priest had been smuggled up the back stairs by James, and Charles II died a Catholic.

James, aware that there was considerable opposition to him and that several alternative Protestant successions were under consideration, turned his thoughts to Ireland. Although relatively little land now remained in Irish hands, the population was overwhelmingly Catholic, and consequently the country could be regarded either as a place of refuge, if the worst came to the worst, or a base from which he might attempt the reconquest of his kingdom. Within six months of his accession, James had broken the Test Acts — measures designed to prevent any man from holding an official post or the king's commission without first declaring his disbelief in transubstantiation, the Catholic dogma which insists that the bread and wine used in the ceremony of Holy Communion are factually and not symbolically transformed by the priest into the actual body and blood of Christ.

Ignoring the Test Acts, James gave a regiment of horse to Dick Talbot; he later became Earl of Tyrconnel and is much better known simply as Tyrconnel. Talbot, a descendant of an old 'degenerate' Anglo-Norman family and the brother of a former Catholic Archbishop of Dublin, had settled in Leinster and was a devout Catholic. He had met James in Flanders and was a favourite at court where he made no secret of his own particular brand of patriotism and where he frequently argued the case for the restoration of the land confiscated from his compatriots. He was one of the few survivors of the siege of Drogheda, which not unnaturally coloured his whole outlook. Drogheda, on the mouth of the River Boyne about thirty miles north of Dublin, was systematically sacked in 1649 by Cromwell to teach the Irish a lesson and to punish them for taking the wrong side in the civil war. It was the first Irish town invested by Cromwell when he arrived in Ireland shortly after the execution of Charles I, and there he allowed his soldiers to massacre 3,000 of the inhabitants, men, women and children, despite the fact that they had been promised quarter. Talbot was serving in Drogheda at the time and had witnessed this massacre. James created Talbot Earl of Tyrconnel in 1685, and allowed him in effect to take command of the army in Ireland. Right from the outset, Tyrconnel behaved as if he had been made Viceroy. When, in 1685, Ormonde* the Lord Lieutenant went to England to see James, the government of Ireland was entrusted to the two Lords Justice, the Primate and the Earl of Granard, who was titular Commander-in-Chief of the Army in Ireland. Tyrconnel ignored Granard and started to make plans for the transformation of the army, which was about 7,000 strong, into a predominantly Catholic force.

James was well aware of the danger inherent in ever allowing a native like Tyrconnel to become Viceroy – the danger was, of course, that a native Viceroy might without much difficulty turn himself into an independent sovereign – so he decided to divide the administration, leaving Tyrconnel in charge of military matters in Ireland, and appointing his own brother-in-law, Clarendon, an Anglican, as Lord Lieutenant, to look after the civil

---

*Sometimes spelt Ormond, just at Tyrconnel is sometimes spelt Tyrconnell. This uncertainty applies to most of the proper names mentioned in the book; the *Dictionary of National Biography* lists three spellings – Michelborne, Mitchelburn and Mitchelburne – for one of the Governors of Londonderry. In those days apparently, people were not very consistent about the spelling of their names – any more, indeed, than they were in Shakespeare's day. I have taken what seems to be the most widely used version in each case.

administration, to the great disappointment of Irish Catholics and presumably of Tyrconnel himself. But even after the appointment of Clarendon, Tyrconnel, often from Whitehall, exercised far more power than was his prerogative. In effect, Clarendon soon found himself a subordinate in the administration he had expected to lead because Tyrconnel was influencing policy. Clarendon found that he was being informed of changes which were to be made in the civil and military government in Ireland above his head, and was told that it was planned to bring a large number of Catholics into office. At this news, landowners sold their estates, traders wound up their business and many English prepared to leave Ireland. The revenue was affected. Preparations were being made, it was said, to enlist and drill the entire Catholic population of Ireland, and Tyrconnel was believed to be directing operations from London, using parish priests as recruiting officers.

In June 1686 Tyrconnel arrived in Dublin and soon openly took the government of Ireland into his hands, as well as the reorganization of the army. He had already angered the Protestant gentry by interpreting a general order to disarm the population as referring specifically to the English, who greatly resented not being allowed to keep a brace of pistols in the house with which to defend themselves against the savage Irish peasants whom they felt to be on the brink of revolt. In much the same way, an American WASP from the southern states today would resent being deprived of the right to keep a revolver under the pillow against the day when the Negroes would rise up in revolt.

As effective Commander-in-Chief in the Army, Tyrconnel now set about reorganizing it in earnest. Protestant officers were sacked at his whim and those who lost their commissions — for which they had paid dearly — were not automatically recompensed but had to go to Dublin at their own expense to press their claims. As for the rank and file, there were stories, probably exaggerated, of foot soldiers, stripped of the uniform for which they had paid, and troopers bereft of their horses and even of their boots, being obliged to walk barefoot to their homes or to the houses of their friends. Most of them, it was said, got no compensation for their horses, uniforms, boots or any arrears of pay owed. Between 200 and 300 Protestant gentlemen who had paid out large sums of money for their commissions were thus deprived of a part of their fortunes while between 5,000 and 6,000 soldiers were sent packing. They were all replaced by Catholics, and the Catholic officers rode the horses paid for by the Protestant officers who had lost their commissions.

By the end of 1687 the reconstruction of the Irish army was complete; and some of the officers had been recruited from the lowest ranks of the Irish population. These newly commissioned officers, many of them descendants of men who had taken part in the 1641 rising, were not given any pay or subsistence for their men for three months and consequently they allowed their troops to live off the country by looting. The arms which had been taken from the Protestants were distributed among these soldiers who were encouraged to raid other houses for arms and ammunition, and not unnaturally these searches for hidden arms became an excuse for further plundering.

In addition, it was still everywhere believed that Irish Catholic civilians were being armed and that the priests would not allow the men to come to Mass unless armed with a skean — a short, dagger-like knife — or half-pike. This may or may not have been true; in more recent years, even when the Irish were being sorely oppressed, the priests always remained resolutely on the side of the establishment. But it is not surprising that these rumours were causing increasing anxiety among the settlers in Ulster.

Not content with acting over the head of Clarendon, the Lord Lieutenant in Ireland, Tyrconnel was constantly conspiring against him in Whitehall, with the result that by the autumn of 1686 he had managed to persuade James to replace Clarendon. James remained, however, resolutely against the idea of giving the title of Lord Lieutenant or Viceroy to an Irishman, and instead made Tyrconnel Lord Deputy, a much inferior title. He was sworn in on 12 February 1687.

Clarendon's departure was followed by a mass emigration of Protestant gentlemen, merchants, traders and artificers; about 1,500 families emigrated in the course of a few days.

Now that he had transferred the military power in Ireland into Catholic hands, Tyrconnel turned his attention to the civil administration. He transferred the office of Attorney General from a Protestant to a Catholic and left only three Protestants on the Bench. Catholic revenue officers were appointed all over the country, and of the sheriffs appointed in 1687, only one was a Protestant – Charles Hamilton of Donegal, selected, it was said, only as a result of confusing him with another man of the same name who was in fact a Catholic. The two sheriffs for Londonderry, appointed by charter, remained Protestants.

Next Tyrconnel began to recall civic charters and to appoint new and predominantly Catholic corporations. The first move was against Dublin Corporation, and Londonderry came next, though the move was strenuously resisted by a party there under the leadership of Robert Rochfort, the Recorder. A charter dated 3 August 1687 elected a new Corporation for Londonderry consisting of a Mayor, twenty aldermen, forty burgesses, two sheriffs, a recorder and a chamberlain. This was a predominantly Catholic Corporation but some Protestants were included in it, among them Henry Campsie who later became the leader of the party of Apprentice Boys who closed the City gates in the face of King James's troops. There were probably only about twenty Protestants in all in Tyrconnel's Corporation. Until then, the Corporation of Londonderry had always been entirely Protestant and one of its decrees had been that no Papist should live within the walls; Catholics had their homes outside the walls, in the suburbs and in the area now known as the Bogside.

The old Corporation simply refused to recognize the existence of the new one and continued to meet as usual as if the latter did not exist. If the Catholic Corporation ever did meet, no minutes of its proceedings survive. It certainly never met after the closing of Londonderry's gates in December 1688.

At about the same time Tyrconnel began to attack the Act of Settlement and to demand that their former lands should be given back to the dispossessed Irish. King James and his Catholic supporters were nervous about this. They did not want to undo what was one of England's most ambitious plantations, nor did King James want to risk upsetting the many relatives and friends of the settlers in England. But the settlers themselves were not greatly reassured by this; they feared that a House of Commons might be elected in Ireland which would abrogate the Acts of Settlement and turn them all off their lands.

They had every reason to fear, for at this period Parliament was for all practical purposes hand-picked by the administration.

The first Irish Parliament was convoked, as we have seen, towards the end of the thirteenth century; it was no more than an assembly of Anglo-Norman barons who were invited to join the existing council of ecclesiastical and lay peers. No Irish were invited and all business was done in English and French.

When Richard II came to Ireland in 1394 he established an 'English land' – later known as the Pale* – east of a line drawn from Dundalk to the Boyne and down the Barrow to Waterford, and initially it was almost exclusively from this area that members of the Irish Parliaments were drawn.

By the time of the Wars of the Roses, despite the legislation introduced to prevent the Anglo-Norman settlers from degenerating into mere Irish, Ireland had become sufficiently independent for one of the leading Anglo-Norman chiefs, the Earl of Desmond, to defy England by recognizing Irish laws and Irish chieftains and his son went so far as to bring some Irish chiefs to Dublin for the 1464 Parliament.

And by the time of Henry VII, the Anglo-Irish feudal lords were identifying themselves so closely with Irish interests that an Act called Poynings' Law – after the man who introduced it – was passed ensuring that Irish Parliaments could not initiate legislation without the approval of the King and privy council in England.

---

*By the middle of the fifteenth century and thereafter the Pale was reduced to the four counties of Meath, Louth, Dublin and Kildare. Its boundary naturally fluctuated with the fortunes of the English settlers in Ireland.

The Irish Parliament which declared Henry VIII King of Ireland in 1541 was a fuller one than had ever met before; it included four archbishops, nineteen bishops and twenty peers as well as deputies representing the 'English land' in Ireland. Henry set up in Ireland all the trappings of the English monarchy, with a royal great seal, a privy council and courts of law on the English pattern, but it was still government controlled from England through the Viceroy.

The Reformation Parliament of 1560 — summoned to put the reformed faith on a constitutional basis — represented ten counties and twenty-eight towns — Ulster and Connaught were unrepresented save for one town deputy from Ulster and two from Connaught. Another Parliament called by Lord Deputy Perrot met in 1585; by now twenty-seven 'shires' or counties and thirty-one towns were returning a total of 118 deputies to the Commons, though Ulster and Connaught were still not represented.

By the time Chichester's Parliament was convened in 1613 to confirm the Ulster plantations and to regularize the introduction of English law throughout Ireland, all Ireland was represented by a total of 232 deputies; the peers at this stage were mainly the old English Catholics from the Pale. Catholics were not debarred but a Protestant majority was secured by 'management' — through the influence of the sheriffs on the strictly limited electorate and by the creation of thirty-nine new boroughs all returning Protestant deputies.

The Parliament which met in 1634 was different; the peers included twenty-four Anglican bishops and the Catholic peers were now out-numbered by the many newly-created Protestant peers.

Cromwell abolished the Irish Parliament and gave the Irish representation in an all-British legislature but the settlers were by now so thoroughly convinced of the advantages of an Irish-based parliament that after Cromwell's departure from the scene, they called a convention in Dublin which reasserted Ireland's right to her own Parliament. This was granted by Charles II though Poyning's Law remained in force.

By now, Irish Parliaments loosely followed the British pattern, with an upper house of peers and bishops and a lower house elected on a very limited franchise – so limited in fact that votes could very easily be controlled. Like the English Parliament, it was only convened sporadically and for specific purposes; at other times the country was administered by the King's representative or Viceroy, variously known as Lord Lieutenant or Lord Deputy according to the rank or power vested in him, with a privy council of picked advisers.

The 'Patriot Parliament' summoned by King James in 1689 was the last legislative assembly of the older Irish race until 1919, and the last until then in which the Catholic faith was represented. It was attended by fifty peers and 230 members of the Commons representing the whole country.

By 1688 Catholics had replaced Protestants in most of the chief administrative posts. Alexander Fitton, a convert to Catholicism, was Lord Chancellor. Thomas Nugent was Chief Justice and Stephen Rice, another Catholic, was Chief Baron of the Exchequer. The Attorney General was Sir Richard Nagle, who had been educated by the Jesuits. In the space of a few months the civil power had been transferred from the settlers to the Celtic population or to the descendants of the 'degenerate' English. The Army had been completely remodelled and many of the 6,000 Protestant veterans who had been dismissed had emigrated and joined King William's armies on the continent.

Although many Protestants emigrated to England, the bulk of them, particularly in Ulster, stayed on, viewing with increasing concern the developments which were taking place and which seemed to be threatening their religion and the very constitution under which they were living.

According to some reports, the Catholics were making increasingly menacing noises. Mass was being said every day in the market places, and it was rumoured that at these Masses the priests were openly talking of the great plans that were afoot which would affect the whole nation. An air of almost deliberate mystery and mistrust seems to have been created and there was talk that Catholics everywhere were being urged to arm themselves 'against the day'. Many of the Catholic laity seem openly to have boasted about the proposed plans, and the feeling began to grow among the

Protestants that another 1641 was at hand — this time with a Catholic king on the throne of England and a Catholic Lord Deputy in charge of Ireland, with a Catholic army at his command and a Catholic administration and judiciary. Irish blacksmiths were reported to be busy making skeans and half-pikes, and even the young boys were believed to be armed. Whether these rumours had any basis is perhaps less important than the fact that the Ulster Protestants believed every word of them and grew hourly more anxious as 'the day' approached.

The landing of William of Orange at Torbay on Guy Fawkes Day in 1688 at the invitation of a powerful party in England determined to overthrow King James II and secure the Protestant succession should have put heart into the Ulster settlers, but William was still far away on the south coast of England and had not yet been accepted by the bulk of the English people.

Around this time, too, a number of anonymous letters were sent to leading citizens and copies were made and circulated, specifically mentioning 9 December 1688 as the date on which the long-awaited massacre was to commence. At Comber, Co. Down, an unsigned and badly-written letter — typical of many that were then circulating — was addressed to the Protestant Earl of Mount-Alexander. Dated 3 December 1688, it read as follows:

> Good my Lord.
> I have written to let you know, that all our Irish men through Ireland is sworn, that on the ninth day of this month, they are to fall on and kill and murder man, wife and child: and I desire your Lordship to take care of yourself and all others that are judged by our men to be heads, for whosoever of them can kill any of you, they are to have a captain's place: so my desire to your honour is to look to yourself, and to give other noblemen warning, and go not out either night or day without a good guard with you, and let no Irish man come near you, whatsoever he be; so this is all from him who is your father's friend, and will be, though I dare not be known, as yet, for fear of my life.

This was only one of many such letters circulated. It is widely accepted now that they were a hoax, though there is no general agreement as to who carried out the hoax, or why. The letters could have been the work of Protestant extremists who thought that those Protestants who felt they had a natural loyalty to the hereditary king, James II, despite his religion, needed some stimulus to make them change their attitude. Or they could have been an attempt on the part of the native Irish further to demoralize the Protestant settlers in the hope that more of them would be encouraged to emigrate and vacate former Irish lands. The strongest evidence that they were a hoax lies in the fact that on 9 December nothing out of the ordinary happened, nor was there any evidence of an aborted uprising. It is possible, of course, that when it became known that a number of these letters had been released, the planned uprising was called off, though it remains probable that some evidence of a projected uprising would have been discovered.

However, so far as the siege of Londonderry is concerned, the important fact is that on top of all the other disquieting news of what Tyrconnel had been doing to the army and to the civil administration in Ireland, at least two copies of letters such as the above reached the city early in December, and the citizens believed that another massacre of 1641 was about to take place on 9 December 1688.

King James II

THE SEVERAL

INFORMATIONS

OF

JOHN MAC-NAMARRA,
MAURICE FITZGERRALD, Gent.
AND
JAMES NASH:

Relating to the HORRID

Popish Plot

IN

IRELAND:

Together with the

RESOLUTIONS

Of the COMMONS in

PARLIAMENT.

Upon the said INFORMATIONS
and MESSAGE from the Lords Spiritual and
Temporal in Parliament.

Thursday the 6th. of January. 1680.

LONDON,

Printed for *John Wright*, at the Crown on *Ludgate-hill*,
and *Richard Chiswell*, at the Rose and Crown in S. *Paul's*
Church-Yard. 1680.

Above left King James landing at Kinsale on 12 March 1689. *Right* An example of one of the many pamphlets that were circulating in the British Isles in the early 1680s, drawing public attention to alleged Popish plots to massacre the Protestants in Ireland.

THE

MESSAGE

FROM THE

Lords to the *Commons.*

January the 4th. 1680.

Resolved,

BY the Lords Spiritual and Temporal, and in Parliament Assembled, That they do declare that they are fully satisfied that there now is, and for divers years last past there hath been, a Horrid and Treasonable Plot and Conspiracy contrived and carried on by those of the *Popish* Religion in *Ireland*, for Massacreing the *English* and Subverting the *Protestant* Religion, and the ancient establish'd Government of that Kingdom, to which their Lordships desire the Concurrence of this House.

The Resolution of the *Commons*, upon the Consideration of the said Message.

January the 6th. 1680.

Resolved,

THat this House doth agree with the Lords in the said *Vote* with the addition of these words, *That the Duke of York being a Papist, and the expectation of his coming to the Crown hath given the greatest Countenance and Encouragement thereto, as well as to the Horrid* Popish Plot in this *Kingdome* of England.

FINIS.

Above left A facsimile of a page from the Commons Journals of the period, giving the terms of a message from the Lords to the Commons on the subject of these threats, and the subsequent Commons resolution. *Right* A view of Londonderry, *circa* 1680, from the north. Shipquay Gate is on the left, beside the jetty. The Bogside is on the extreme right of the picture, and the windmill—which cannot be seen in this drawing—is on the far slope of the hill, behind the cathedral.

Richard Talbot, first Duke of Tyrconnel, who was made Lord Deputy of Ireland by King James in February 1687. He was the man responsible for reorganizing the Irish army, replacing Protestant officers with Catholics and turning it into a predominantly Catholic force.

Lord Mountjoy, a Protestant in very good standing with the inhabitants of Londonderry, who was sent to the city by Tyrconnel to try to persuade it to capitulate. He was later sent to France and imprisoned in the Bastille.

III   *The closing of the gates*

In the years between the Flight of the Earls and the Bloodless Revolution in England, the city of Londonderry had become a prosperous centre of trade and commerce. It will be remembered that when the preparations for the Plantation were under way, the city had been burnt down and the inhabitants slaughtered by Sir Cahir O'Doherty in an unsuccessful revolt. The insurgents were put down, arrangements were completed between the City of London and the Crown for the development of the area, and King James made over to the Guilds of the City of London, in their corporate capacity, the area covered by the old city of Derry and about six thousand acres in its immediate vicinity.

Let Macaulay take up the tale:

> This country, then cultivated and uninhabited, is now enriched with industry, embellished by taste, and pleasing even to eyes accustomed to the well-tilled fields and stately manor houses of England. A new city soon arose which, on account of its connection with the capital of the empire, was called Londonderry. The buildings covered the summit and slope of a hill which overlooked the broad stream of the Foyle, then whitened by vast flocks of wild swans. On the highest ground stood the Cathedral, a church which, though erected when the secret of Gothic architecture was lost, and though ill qualified to sustain a comparison with the awful temples of the middle ages, is not without grace and dignity. Near the Cathedral rose the Palace of the Bishop, whose see was one of the most valuable in Ireland. The city was in form nearly an ellipse; and the principal streets formed a cross, the arms of which met in a square called the Diamond. The original houses have either been rebuilt or so much repaired that their ancient character can no longer be traced; but many of them were standing within living memory. They were in general two stories in height; and some of them had stone staircases on the outside.

The dwellings were encompassed by a wall of which the whole circumference was little less than a mile. On the bastions were placed culverins [ancient cannons of great length, generally 18-pounders, weighing about 50 cwt.] and sakers [small cannons] presented by the wealthy guilds of London to the colony ... The inhabitants were Protestants of Anglo-Saxon blood. They were indeed not all of one country or of one church: but Englishmen and Scotchmen, Episcopalians and Presbyterians, seem to have generally lived together in friendship, a friendship which is sufficiently explained by their common antipathy to the Irish race and to the Popish religion. During the rebellion of 1641, Londonderry had resolutely held out against the native chieftains and had been repeatedly besieged in vain. Since the Restoration [of the monarchy] the city had prospered. The Foyle, when the tide was high, brought up ships of large burden to the quay. The fisheries throve greatly ... the quantity of salmon caught annually was estimated at eleven hundred thousand pounds weight.

The people of Londonderry shared in the alarm which, towards the close of the year 1688, was general among the Protestants settled in Ireland. It was known that the aboriginal peasantry of the neighbourhood were laying in pikes and knives. Priests had been haranguing in a style of which, it must be owned, the Puritan part of the Anglo-Saxon community had little right to complain [a reference to the fact that Cromwell was noted for his extremely free readings from the Old Testament in defence of his worst excesses] about the slaughter of the Amalekites, and the judgements which Saul had brought on himself by sparing one of the proscribed race. Rumours from various quarters and anonymous letters in various hands agreed in naming the ninth of December as the day fixed for the extirpation of the strangers.

While these rumours were circulating in the city, a new crisis developed. For a number of years Lord Mountjoy's Regiment of Foot had been garrisoned in Londonderry. He was a Protestant, as were a number of his officers who included Lieutenant-Colonel Robert Lundy, later Governor of the city. The regiment had escaped the purging which the other regiments in Ireland had suffered at the hands of Tyrconnel, largely because of the high regard in which Mountjoy was everywhere held, and the citizens of Londonderry looked to Mountjoy's regiment for protection against the long-feared Catholic attack.

Now, without warning, Tyrconnel ordered Mountjoy's regiment to quit Londonderry and march to Dublin; he intended to send them for service in England. At the same time he gave orders for the raising of new regiments in each of the four provinces, and put the Earl of Antrim, a Scots Catholic whose family name was MacDonnell, in charge of the new regiment to be raised in Ulster. It was to consist entirely of Irish troops and Scots Highlanders, all Catholics. They were originally to have been equipped and ready to march by 20 November and if they had been ready, would have replaced Mountjoy's regiment before it left Londonderry on 23 November. There was, however, a delay of a fortnight which in the event proved crucial.

One of the reasons for the delay was that the Earl of Antrim, an old man of seventy, was anxious to build around himself a fine-looking body of men, and made it a condition of recruitment that every member of his regiment should be around six feet tall. This took some time to organize, with the result that Londonderry was left without a garrison just at the very moment when these disturbing rumours of an impending massacre on 9 December reached the city. Another reason for Antrim's difficulty in finding recruits for his regiment was the fact that it was generally believed that this regiment, too, was ultimately destined for service in England, and the Irish had no desire to serve on English soil.

In any event, a critical delay of a fortnight occurred. If Mountjoy had remained in the garrison and had handed over to Antrim's troops, the citizens of Londonderry would have had no alternative but to accept the situation. But with time to think about it, they managed to convince themselves that Antrim's troops were part of the overall plan to murder the Protestants.

When Mountjoy left, John Buchanan, the Deputy Mayor, took over control of the town; the Mayor, Cormack O'Neill, a Tyrconnel appointment, had left to join Tyrconnel's army. By now, Antrim's troops were well on the way and had got as far as Limavady when the letters arrived naming 9 December as 'the day'.

Colonel George Phillips, a former Governor of

Londonderry, who was now living outside the city, received one of these letters and sent a messenger to Alderman Norman of Londonderry urging him 'to consult the sober people of the town and set out to them the danger of admitting such guests among them'. The 'guests' were, of course, Antrim's troops; Phillips was convinced that they were part of the plan to extirpate the Protestants.

Antrim's regiment consisted of about 1,200 men, with many camp followers – women and young boys who followed in the hope of sharing some of the spoils – and as anxiety among the Protestants mounted, Colonel Phillips sent another message advising that the gates of Londonderry should be closed in the face of this army and assuring the Deputy Mayor that he and many of his friends from the surrounding countryside would be with the Derry people the following day and would give them every support. The messenger who brought this letter reported that he had passed the advance party of Antrim's Catholic troops about two miles from Londonderry and that the rest were on the march.

Very shortly three companies, comprising about 150 men, arrived on the right bank of the Foyle opposite Londonderry's Ferryquay Gate; the date was 7 December. Two of the officers were ferried across the river and demanded quarters for their men and forage for their horses. As it happened, the warrants they held were unsigned due to an oversight, and this technicality gave the sheriffs a bit of extra time to consider the situation.

In the meantime, news of the letters and of Colonel Phillips's warnings that the city gates should be closed in the face of Antrim's troops began to circulate among the townspeople, with the result that the mobs were soon out in the streets convinced that the second Massacre of the Protestants was at hand and that they had been singled out for the first attack. In general the older people were very hesitant about taking such a step as to close the gates of the city against the King's army – it was, after all, treason, as King James II was still the legitimate ruler – but the younger, wilder element would not listen to reason; they were all for closing the gates and chancing the consequences.

It was now recalled that some years earlier a former councillor of the city, David Cairnes, a prominent lawyer, had warned the citizens to be prepared for the worst and had suggested that if and when it happened, the best course of action would be for them to take the law into their own hands and guard the gates of their city. His advice was now freely quoted, and there doesn't seem to be much doubt that on reflection a good many of the older and wiser inhabitants secretly approved the decision to slam the gates in the face of Antrim's troops – provided that they were not openly associated with the action and that it could afterwards be put down to the hot-headed behaviour of the rabble. The Rev. John Mackenzie, chaplain to one of the regiments during the siege, who wrote about it shortly afterwards in his *Narrative of the Siege of Londonderry*, puts it this way: 'However, divers of those who made some figure in the town wished the thing were done, yet none of them thought fit to be themselves active in it.'

At first it was thought that Antrim's troops would spend the night on the far side of the river and attempt to enter the city in the morning, and the debate as to what should be done was still going on when it was observed that the vanguard of the regiment had started to cross the river by ferry, and was moving towards a landing place near the Ferryquay Gate, a distance of about 300 yards from the walls of the city.

It was at this moment that the apprentice youths made their fateful decision, a decision which, according to C.D. Milligan's *History of the Siege of Londonderry, 1689,* was 'to prove momentous for Protestantism in Ireland, important for the future of England and Scotland and fatal for James'.

It was coming up to noon on 7 December 1688 when, as the Catholic troops approached the gate, the apprentice boys drew their swords, ran to the main guard, seized the keys – there was not, it seems, much determined opposition to their action – rushed to the Ferryquay Gate, drew up the drawbridge, and locked the gates. Lord Antrim's forces were within sixty yards of the gate when the drawbridge was drawn up in their faces. The apprentice boys then hurried around the other three gates of the city, Bishop's Gate,

Butcher's Gate and Shipquay Gate, and locked them too. Mackenzie names thirteen apprentice boys, though he says that there were others involved in this escapade. The boys were apprentices to the various London Guilds which had set up branches in Londonderry, and could have been aged between fourteen and about twenty. They were probably in their late teens.

Antrim's men stood about dumbfounded, uncertain what to do next, more especially as they knew that two of their officers were inside the walls trying to arrange for their accommodation. It was at this stage that James Morrison, a citizen of Londonderry who was on the ramparts near the Ferryquay Gate when it was closed, shouted to them to go away. When the soldiers continued to hesitate, he called: 'Bring about a great gun here', and this, according to all accounts, settled the matter. Antrim's troops made their way back to the ferry and crossed over to the far side of the river.

William King, an archbishop of Dublin, and author of *The State of the Protestants of Ireland under the late King James's Government* (published in 1691), claims that Antrim's soldiers appeared before the city without the King's livery, without any officers of note or the least warning from the Earl of Tyrconnel as to their coming, and he further asserts that they were armed like a rabble, with skeans, clubs and such weapons as the Rapparees and Tories used. (The Rapparees and Tories were secret Catholic agrarian armies which carried out raids on Protestant farms and homesteads by night; they had their Protestant counterparts.) King goes further and claims that the people of Londonderry would have been false to their charter if they had given the city over to those very people the charter had designed it to be a bulwark against. There was no reason, he argued, why they should deliver it up to a parcel of men of whose commission they knew nothing and whose intention, they believed, was to cut their throats.

But this very valid argument was thought up later, with the aid of hindsight; at the time there were many people in Londonderry wondering anxiously if they had done the right thing in treasonably locking the gates in the face of the forces of the King.

However, with the gates of Londonderry closed against Antrim's troops, the die had been cast so far as the city was concerned, and the important thing now was to decide what was to be done next. The young apprentice boys had no doubts about this. They had noticed that the two officers from Antrim's regiment and the Deputy Mayor had sent a party to secure the armoury, so they immediately hurried off to the magazine to seize it themselves. When they arrived, led by Henry Campsie, the sentinel – a man called Linegar and a Catholic as it so happened – half-heartedly attempted to defend the magazine and in the process fired a shot, slightly wounding Campsie. It was only a superficial graze, but it gave the Protestants their first martyr. Linegar was seized and locked up in jail. The older people of the city, though they secretly approved of this action too, were fully aware that Linegar had merely been doing his duty, and feared reprisals by Tyrconnel. The Deputy Mayor, the sheriffs, the two officers from Antrim's regiment and a number of prominent Protestants went to the market place to try to persuade those who had shut the gates to open them again – which they could have done without any danger, since Antrim's troops were now on the far side of the river – but the apprentice boys and their supporters were determined to hold the city.

To call them the apprentice boys' *supporters* is perhaps misleading; it would be more accurate to say that by now a good many of the ordinary citizens – the Protestant, mainly working-class element – were openly supporting the action of the boys in closing the gates. It seems probable, too, that many of the clergymen, officers and burghers were also in favour of their action, though less openly; and it could be that their gesture in going to the market place to urge that the gates be re-opened was merely a move to avoid reprisals later, if King James's army should return and capture the city.

In the absence of any statistics on the subject, it is only possible to guess at the social and religious structure of the city at this stage. Normally, at the top, there would have been a stratum composed of the clergymen of the established church – the Church of Ireland, an institution similar to the Church of England, with the King as titular head, and financed, like the Church of England, out of tithes collected regardless of denomination or religion from all property-owners – the merchants and burghers and the gentry (who would almost all have been Church of Ireland). Next there would have been a preponderance of small shop-keepers, tradesmen, minor officials and of course the workers in the various guilds; they would have been largely non-Conformist. Mackenzie lists seventeen established church and eight non-Conformist clergymen as electing to stay on in Londonderry during the siege; but the figures would not reflect a comparable ratio in the congregations, for the established church, being the established church, could afford a higher proportion of priests to people, a matter which caused great resentment among the non-Conformists in times of less stress. Finally, there would have been a small group of Catholics doing the most menial of tasks, for despite all the bans and regulations a small number of Catholics seems to have remained in Londonderry throughout the siege.

This pattern was probably upset by the number of refugees in the city – there were more and more, as the days passed – from the surrounding countryside, many of whom would have been small farmers and farm labourers, mostly non-Conformist, but containing a fair percentage of Church of Ireland members.

There were continuous meetings throughout the day, and in the evening a meeting of Protestants was held in the Town Hall. It was attended by the Deputy Mayor, members of the Corporation, Dr Ezekiel Hopkins (the Bishop of Derry), and other prominent citizens. The Deputy Mayor was in favour of receiving Antrim's regiment into the town, and he assured his audience that if they did so, all would be well. Dr Hopkins, who, like most churchmen, was a firm believer in the Divine Right of Kings, favoured submission to Tyrconnel as the King's deputy. An alderman called Gervais Squire held that to admit Antrim's troops would make them traitors to the liberty of the citizens and to the charter of the city. The Bishop was trying to reply to this when a man called Alexander Irwin interrupted. 'Your sermon is very good, but we haven't time to listen to it now,' he said. (Another version has it that he said: 'My lord, your doctrine is very good, but we can't now hear you out.') The assembly was firmly resolved to resist, and the Bishop made no impression on them; he left the next day for Raphoe, and thence to England.

As soon as David Cairnes — the former councillor who had urged the closing of the gates some years earlier and who was now living outside the city — heard rumours of the threatened massacre, he hurried to Londonderry, arriving shortly after the gates had been shut. They were opened again for him and he expressed his warm approval of the action of the apprentice boys and congratulated them, before going on a tour of the walls to encourage the guards and sentinels. He also used his great influence with the more faint-hearted of the respectable and influential citizens, and gradually the tide of public favour began to turn openly in favour of the action of the apprentice boys. That night David Cairnes, Alderman Norman and a number of the other leading citizens had a discussion on the best means to defend the city and sent out letters to other members of the Protestant gentry living in the neighbourhood, telling them what had happened and pointing out to them the need for a concerted policy for their mutual defence and safety. In the course of the next few days there were varied replies, some of them promising support, others expressing disapproval.

But expressions of disapproval, wherever they came from, could no longer stem the turn that events were now taking in Londonderry. Guards were posted inside and outside the walls, the magazine was broken open and muskets and a supply of powder were taken out and distributed among the city's defenders. Protestants from the surrounding area began to crowd into Londonderry with stories of the rough behaviour of Antrim's troops, now quartered on the other side of the River Foyle.

There had also been a considerable exodus from the city and it was feared that there were not more than about 300 men capable of bearing arms. On the other hand, it was reckoned that there were at least as many again in the suburbs immediately outside the walls, and the citizens were hourly expecting assistance from Protestants living in the area around the city.

On the morning of 9 December, the day that was to have marked the start of the massacre, nothing happened except that news reached Londonderry that King James's daughter Anne, Princess of Denmark (the future Queen Anne of England), had given her support to William's cause. This news was greeted by firing two of the great guns.

As King William had marched westwards from Torbay, where he landed on 5 November, towards London, more and more of England's prominent families and many of James's former generals and courtiers went over to his side — including the best officer in James's army, Lord Churchill, later the Duke of Marlborough. Long before William reached London it was clear that he was in undisputed control of the country; the only question that now remained was to find a formula by which he could be constitutionally crowned king. With every day that passed, James's hope of regaining his kingdom was diminishing. The news that his younger daughter Anne had given her blessing to William's cause must have seemed like the final straw; his elder daughter Mary was, after all, married to William of Orange and would owe her first loyalty to her husband.

About this time a considerable body of armed men arrived in Londonderry; one detachment had been sent by Alderman Tomkins, with his son John as Captain. Alderman Tomkins, like a good many members of the Londonderry Corporation, lived outside the city, and when the news of its defiant stand reached them, they began to collect around them the private armies they had been raising to defend themselves against the expected Catholic attack. These they now marched to the assistance of Londonderry.

In fact, from this time forward until the end of the siege, endless parties of Protestant refugees, some of them useful fighting men, others just so many more hungry mouths to feed, kept continuously arriving in the city. And although the impression gained from many brief accounts of the siege is that the gates of Londonderry were locked by the apprentice boys on 7 December and thereafter were not opened again until after the relief of the city, there was constant traffic in and out of Londonderry, not only during the 'phoney' siege which preceded the siege proper, but even when the city was in its final extremity.

The Earl of Antrim had himself now reached Newtown Limavady and was lodging there on the night of 8 December with George Phillips, the former Governor of Londonderry, before continuing on to Londonderry the next day. (Antrim, of course, had no idea that Phillips's loyalties were with the Londonderry citizens). Before he arrived, however, the citizens of Londonderry had taken their first offensive action. Shots were fired from the city walls at Antrim's troops while a party of fifty or sixty boys under George Cook drew up on the shore, outside the walls, near Ferryquay Gate, where they were mistaken by the Irish troops for Laganeers, a Protestant force famous for their victories over the Irish Catholic rebels in 1641. At the same time Tomkins appeared on a hill near Antrim's men with some thirty or forty horse, and Antrim's soldiers fled, leaving their coats and in some cases even their boots behind them.

The fleeing troops encountered the Earl of Antrim about a mile from the city and told him what had happened. He was travelling in a coach with George Phillips. Antrim now sent Phillips ahead to find out who was in charge of Londonderry and whether he would be admitted. Phillips, coming from the enemy, had at first some difficulty in getting into the city, but when he made it clear who he was and that all his sympathies lay with the citizens, he was admitted and received by David Cairnes who had temporarily taken command.

He asked Phillips to make it look as if he were being held in Londonderry by force, against his will. This was done; Phillips sent a message to Antrim explaining that he had been taken prisoner and advising Antrim not to continue into the city.

The Earl of Antrim — not sure that he was strong enough to take the city and not wanting to start what amounted to a sort of civil war without higher authority — retired to Coleraine and tried to rally his scattered regiment, eventually falling back as far as Antrim. In Londonderry, Phillips, who had been Governor of Londonderry and the nearby fort of

Culmore in King Charles II's time, and was also a Colonel by rank, was chosen as Governor, with Cairnes's approval. The keys of the city gates and the magazine were handed over to him.

In the meantime the citizens composed a letter to Lord Mountjoy, in Dublin, whom they trusted, explaining what had happened. On 9 December a letter signed by John Campsie, Alderman Norman and others told Mountjoy that a 'rabble' had shut the city gates on some of the Earl of Antrim's troops 'which we then blamed them for, though we could not refrain them'. It was, as C.D. Milligan remarks, a very tactful letter, disclaiming all responsibility for the action of the apprentice boys but reiterating the fears of the Protestants that an attack upon them was imminent and making it quite clear that they were resolved to defend themselves against their enemies in Ulster, whom they believed to be bent on their slaughter. They were perhaps encouraged to send this letter by the knowledge that William of Orange was now marching unopposed on London.

Protestant troops and amateur soldiers from the surrounding countryside continued to trickle into the city to reinforce the garrison. On the day after the letter was sent to Mountjoy, a Captain Forward and a Mr William Stewart brought between 200 and 300 horse into the city, and a Mr Cowan of St Johnston* a whole company of foot. Forward, who had been Sheriff for Co. Donegal in 1688, had received the general command which had gone out from Tyrconnel to disarm all Protestants, but instead of obeying it had imported a supply of arms and ammunition from Holland which he now brought into Londonderry.

The city was, however, still pitifully ill-equipped with the necessary war materials to withstand a siege, and Governor Phillips decided to send David Cairnes to London to see whether he could get any assistance there. Cairnes carried with him a letter to the Irish Society in London – as the association of City Guilds which had undertaken the development of Derry was now called – informing the society of what had happened in terms similar to those in Mountjoy's

---

*Now called St Johnstown

letter. 'But just as the soldiers were approaching the gates,' the letter ran, 'the youth-hood by a strange impulse, ran in one body and shut the gates, and put themselves in the best posture of defence they could. We blamed, but could not guide or persuade them to any less resolution that night; and so the soldiers retired, and were quartered in the neighbour-hood, where, although they did not murder or destroy any, yet many threats they uttered, and outrages they committed. The next day we hoped to prevail with those that assumed the power of the city, to open the gates and receive the garrison; but the news and intimations of the general design came so fast, so full from all quarters, that we then blessed God for our present escape, effected by means unseen and against our wills.' The letter was signed by Governor George Phillips, John Campsie, Samuel Norman, Alexander Tomkins and others.

Before he left, David Cairnes formed the townspeople into six companies of foot under Captains Samuel Norman, Alexander Lecky, Matthew Cocken, Warham Jemmet, John Tomkins and Thomas Moncrieff. The junior officers included five of the apprentice boys.

In addition to the letters sent to Mountjoy and to the Irish Society in London, a declaration in more or less the same terms was now made by the sheriffs and citizens. It said that when a company of Antrim's regiment advanced on the town, the inhabitants regarded themselves as sheep destined for slaughter and thought that Antrim's troops were about to carry out that sentence. 'But,' the declaration went on, 'it pleased the Lord who watcheth over us, so to order things, that when they were ready to enter the city, a great number of the younger and some of the meaner sort of inhabitants, ran hastily to the gates and shut them, loudly denying entrance to such guests and obstinately refusing obedience to us.'

With typical hypocrisy, the leading citizens of Londonderry disassociated themselves from this action on the part of 'the meaner sort of inhabitants' while at the same time taking advantage of it to pursue their own designs which were precisely the same: to keep the Catholic army out of Londonderry. The declaration went on to say that at first the sheriffs and citizens were amazed at such behaviour, but upon information which they later received of a general design upon the Protestants they began to consider it as a special instance of God's mercy towards the citizens that they were not delivered over as a prey to those who conspired against them, 'that it pleased Him to stir up the spirit of the people so unexpectedly to provide for their common safety and preservation.' The declaration, however, made no bones about where the sheriffs and citizens of Londonderry now stood: ' . . . we have resolved to stand upon our guard and to defend our walls, and not to admit any Papishes whatsoever to quarter amongst us.'

Shortly after this, the city was cleared of the majority of Catholics still within the walls and 'a convent of Dominican Friars packed off'. Theoretically, there shouldn't have been any Catholics inside Londonderry's walls, but it was never possible to exclude Catholics altogether, whatever the regulations said. In such matters, above all in Ireland, there were always 'special cases' and it is probable that some Catholics remained in the city right through the siege; just as in Dublin, despite all orders, regulations and proclamations, Catholics continued to live quite openly in the city even during Cromwell's sojourn there.

IV *Now or never! Now and forever!*

When the rumours that the massacre of Protestants was due to begin on 9 December first began to circulate throughout the country, Tyrconnel called the leading Protestants to Dublin and issued an official denial of these rumours, but the emigration which had started when Clarendon was replaced by Tyrconnel continued and indeed increased to such an extent that there was great difficulty in finding accommodation on seaworthy vessels, and many Protestant families entrusted themselves to the hazards of the stormy Irish Sea in small open boats.

The Protestant settlers who decided to stay on in Ireland began to draw ever closer to one another for their mutual safety, and many of the larger country houses were turned into fortresses. On the fateful night of 9 December, there was hardly a Protestant house in which the lights were not left burning all night and most of them had armed men on guard. On that night, as we have seen, nothing untoward happened, but the rumours of the impending uprising continued to fly about, and all over the country gentlemen and yeomen left their country estates and clustered together in those towns which, although they now had Catholic magistrates and sheriffs, nevertheless remained largely in Protestant hands. Sligo, Charleville, Mallow and Bandon were among the Protestant strongholds in the south. Apart from Londonderry, the principal Protestant stronghold in the north was Enniskillen.

Enniskillen at this period was no more than a village — about eighty buildings clustered around an old castle. Early in December 1688, when the citizens heard that two companies of Catholic Irish infantry were to be quartered on them, they decided not to admit these troops. They sent out a message appealing for help from all

Protestants living in the area, and within a few hours a force of about 200 foot and 250 horse had been assembled. Tyrconnel's soldiers, who were already nearing the town, had brought with them supplies of arms. They distributed these among the Irish Catholic peasants who attached themselves to the army in the hope of getting their hands on a share of the booty when the Protestant defenders of the town were defeated.

However, the townsfolk of Enniskillen did not wait to be attacked; instead, they came out themselves and fell upon Tyrconnel's army which, not expecting any resistance, was completely taken by surprise on seeing such a formidable body of foot and cavalry approaching. The peasant camp-followers immediately fled in disorder, and before long the soldiers had followed suit, not pausing until they had reached the safety of Cavan.

The people of Enniskillen, encouraged by this first and easy victory, now set about drawing up plans for the defence of their district. Gustavus Hamilton, one of the officers who had lost his commission when Tyrconnel remodelled the Irish army, was appointed Governor and Commander-in-Chief. The inhabitants continued to enlist help from Protestants in the neighbourhood and set the local blacksmiths to work manufacturing weapons. All the country houses in the district were fortified, and any Catholics still in the town were kept under close surveillance. But Enniskillen was so much smaller and less important than Londonderry — at this period the only sizeable port in the north of Ireland, since Belfast was no more than a collection of mud huts on the banks of the River Lagan — that it did not occupy anything like the same attention on the part of Tyrconnel and his officers.

When the news of Londonderry's stand against his troops reached Tyrconnel, he decided that William Stuart, Viscount Mountjoy, a Protestant in very good standing with the inhabitants of the city, would have the best chance of persuading them to submit. Accordingly, although Mountjoy and his troops had only just arrived in Dublin *from* Londonderry three days earlier after a long and tiring march in the depths of winter, he turned them smartly about and marched them northwards again, with Mountjoy himself and Colonel Robert Lundy in command. Lundy was a professional soldier who had served in Tangiers and elsewhere before being posted to Viscount Mountjoy's regiment in Ireland.

When Mountjoy got as far as Omagh, he sent a Captain McCausland on ahead of his troops into Londonderry with a request that two or three representatives of the citizens should come as far as Raphoe to discuss the situation with him. Captain Samuel Norman, who had been an Alderman on the old Protestant corporation – which was now effectively running the city – and John Mogridge, one of the city burgesses, were chosen to go and hear what Mountjoy had to say.

The two men returned from their visit to Raphoe with the news that Mountjoy was fully empowered to negotiate, and that on the surrender of the garrison and the handing over of their arms, he would procure for them a full and free pardon for everything that had taken place.

However, by this time Governor Phillips was busy arming the citizens – recently formed into companies by David Cairnes – out of the stores. Additional arms were daily being brought into the city by Protestant supporters in the neighbouring area, and consequently the citizens felt that they were in a position to hold out at least until they had received replies to the letter they had sent to England with David Cairnes. Captain Norman and John Mogridge also reported to the sheriffs and citizens of Londonderry that Mountjoy had asked them to see that the city appointed commissioners with plenipotentiary powers to conclude a formal agreement and send these commissioners for further discussions with Mountjoy at Mongevlin Castle, near St Johnston.

Whether the citizens of Londonderry seriously intended to treat with Mountjoy at this stage or whether they were merely playing for extra time, it is impossible to say, but at least they did appoint a commission to go and see Mountjoy. This commission consisted of the Governor, Colonel George Phillips; Captain Alexander Tomkins; Sheriff Horace Kennedy; Lieutenant William Crookshanks, one of the

apprentice boys; and Lieutenant James Lenox. They listened
to his proposals and informed him that they would only
comply on certain conditions. The troops admitted to the
garrison would all have to be Protestants; the city companies
must be permitted to retain their arms and continue to keep
watches; and there should be a free and general pardon under
the Great Seal. Mountjoy was in no way empowered to offer
such generous terms to the rebellious garrison and so the
discussion was abortive. Mountjoy did however tell the
commission that he intended to present himself at the gates
of Londonderry the next morning and demand admittance.

This he duly did, and his action put the inhabitants of
Londonderry into a quandary. He was a Protestant and he
was well-liked in the city. On the other hand, he had come at
the command of the Catholic Lord Deputy, Tyrconnel, and
so the citizens were not disposed to take any chances. After
obliging Mountjoy to kick his heels outside the gates for a
while, during which a heated discussion took place inside, it
was eventually decided to send a deputation of ten
men – including Governor Phillips, Captains Lecky and
Jemmet, Captain Forward and several others, one of them an
apprentice boy – to treat with Mountjoy outside the gates of
the city.

Articles of agreement were eventually drawn up under
which, within fifteen days, Mountjoy would publish a general
pardon under the Great Seal, and until such time only two
companies were to be quartered in the city. These were to be
commanded by Colonel Robert Lundy and Captain William
Stewart. Another condition was that the inhabitants were to
be permitted to retain their arms and keep watches. No
stranger was to be allowed to come within the walls with
firearms, or lodge within the gates, unless authorized by
Lundy or the sheriffs, and if before 1 March Mountjoy's
regiment should be ordered to leave Londonderry, he or his
commanding officer would leave the city free to organize its
own guards and watches.

Although, for a garrison which had openly defied the
authority of the King's deputy, these seem pretty generous
terms, the Rev. George Walker, one of the contemporary
historians of the siege – he was afterwards made a Governor

of the city – appears to feel guilty about treating with Mountjoy at all and advances the excuse that Mountjoy was a Protestant, with the best interests of the garrison at heart, and that furthermore, as former Master of the Ordnance, he must have been well aware that they only had two barrels of powder in the magazine and were in no strong position to defend themselves. Also, there was as yet no sign of the expected assistance from England.

The agreement drawn up between the representatives of the city of Londonderry and Lord Mountjoy contained other provisions. Citizens and their families who wished to leave the city and suburbs with their goods were to be allowed to do so. There was to be no embargo on ships leaving the harbour and if any ship which had sailed from Londonderry since 7 December – the day on which the gates were closed – had been stopped or arrested because of events there, it was to be released immediately. Finally, until 26 March – by which time, presumably, the garrison assumed that assistance would have arrived from England – no troops of Antrim's regiment were to be quartered in the city or its surrounding suburbs. There was a specific clause to protect such civil servants as Warham Jemmet, a customs officer, and other officials who had become involved in the stand against Antrim's army, that no imputation or blame should be attached to them for their 'involuntary compliance' with the people of Londonderry in the action they had taken. As it happened, two of Mountjoy's sons were in Londonderry at this time, and the agreement further stipulated that they would remain in the city as a guarantee until the full terms of the agreement had been duly carried out.

As a first step towards meeting the citizens' terms, Mountjoy ordered Lundy to go to Strabane and quarter his six companies there until he had sifted out his ranks and replaced a number of the Catholics by Protestants. The mistrustful citizens of Londonderry sent a deputation to Strabane to see that this part of the bargain was being faithfully carried out. They also saw to it that the two companies to be admitted to the city consisted entirely of Protestants. The other four companies, about half of whose members were Catholics, were ordered to quarter at

Strabane, Newtownstewart and Raphoe until they had been thoroughly 'reformed'.

Late in December, Lundy's Protestant companies were admitted to Londonderry; whereupon Governor George Phillips resigned and Mountjoy appointed Lundy as Governor in his place. Around this time, the men of Enniskillen sent a deputation to Lundy looking for his support in their stand against Tyrconnel's Irish army, but he advised them to submit to the King's authority. On their return journey, the deputation had an interview with Mountjoy at Newtownstewart. He gave them the same advice. The King, he said, would protect them. Allen Cathcart, one of the emissaries, replied that if all they heard from England was true, the King would have a difficult enough job protecting himself.

By now it was known in Ireland that King James had fled England and was living as a guest of King Louis XIV of France in a palace near Versailles, and that William of Orange had been received in triumph at Westminster and had taken over administration of the realm. There remained, however, the problem of finding a constitutional way of slotting William into the English monarchical succession. A parliament which couldn't actually call itself a parliament because it hadn't been convened by a King and was instead known as the Convention met and decided that with the flight of James the throne of England was now vacant. But it was essential for the principle of legitimate succession that it should never be vacant. This meant accepting either that James was still on the throne or that his infant Catholic son had succeeded him. There were several ways out of this dilemma. The Convention could assume that James's perversity in sticking to the Catholic religion had proved him insane and justified them in appointing William as Regent. They could accept the popular and absurd rumour that the Prince of Wales was an imposter smuggled into the non-pregnant Queen's bed in a warming pan, in which case James's daughter Mary would be the natural heir to the throne, with William as Prince Consort.

William himself settled the matter. He would not be Regent, he said, and he would not, without a royal title, accept a subordinate place at his wife's side. After his death, he was agreeable that the succession should revert to Princess Anne and her descendants. As a compromise, the Convention settled on the idea of a dual monarchy, and in February William and Mary formally accepted the offer of the throne which was made to them jointly.

The articles of agreement between the citizens of Londonderry and Lord Mountjoy are dated 21 December, but Tyrconnel wrote to the Earl of Antrim on 18 December from Dublin Castle, telling him to be prepared to march on Londonderry at short notice, to reduce it. Since Tyrconnel cannot have been unaware of the negotiations into which Mountjoy had entered with the citizens of Londonderry, it must be assumed that he had no intention of honouring them, but merely allowed Mountjoy to proceed with the negotiations in order to gain time. He instructed Antrim to have his regiment ready to march at one hour's notice, and stated that if Londonderry had not submitted by 21 December he would give Antrim orders to march on the city and would appear before the gates himself.

In the event, however, nothing happened; 21 December came and went, and the situation in Londonderry remained unchanged, probably because Tyrconnel now had more on his mind than the reduction of a rebellious seaport in distant Ulster.

The Protestant party in England which had urged William of Orange to take over the throne had recently been urging on him the necessity of doing something about Ireland. He had promised to do his best to maintain the Protestant and English interests there, but for the moment there was little that he could accomplish in practice. The army in England until recently had been ranged against him, and by no means all of its officers and men were reconciled to his succession to the throne. He could not spare the army he had brought with him from Holland; he needed it in England until things settled down. The treasury was empty and the navy was owed arrears of pay, so that he was in no position to commission an army of mercenaries to police Ireland. All he could do at this stage was to express his good intentions.

A great meeting of noblemen and gentlemen with interests

in Ireland was held at the house of the Duke of Ormonde (former Lord Lieutenant in Ireland) in St James's Square, London, and tried to persuade the Prince of Orange to see whether Tyrconnel couldn't be tempted to change over to the Williamite side. Tyrconnel had already professed himself willing to consider such a proposition, and had taken counsel with Mountjoy and others who, although they had not thrown off their allegiance to King James as hereditary ruler of England, nevertheless remained firmly committed to the Protestant faith and the English connection in Ireland. Again, whether Tyrconnel ever seriously considered going over to William's side, or whether he, too, was merely playing for time, it is impossible to say: but it is hard to imagine that an Anglo-Irish Catholic, brother of a former Catholic archbishop of Dublin, who had fought in the siege of Drogheda, could ever seriously have considered coming to terms with the Prince of Orange and the Williamites.

But in England, where so many ancient Catholic families had already gone over to William's cause, it was considered a possibility worth following up. Sir William Temple, the eminent British statesman and diplomat, who had negotiated William of Orange's marriage to King James's daughter, was approached – his family had considerable tracts of property in Ireland and he himself had represented Carlow in Parliament – and he suggested that his own eldest son, John Temple, should be consulted. Through John Temple, Richard Hamilton – a Catholic of Scottish stock who had lived for some time in Ireland – was selected to go to Ireland to try to persuade Tyrconnel to transfer his allegiance from King James II to William of Orange.

Whether Hamilton ever intended to keep his promise or not, he soon found on arrival in Ireland that he had undertaken an impossible task. Tyrconnel had set something in train in Ireland which he could no longer control even if he had wanted to. He had stimulated the Irish into believing that at long last they were about to get their old lands back. When rumours reached them – as they did – that Tyrconnel had been negotiating with William, they threatened to burn down Dublin Castle with him inside it and to put themselves under the protection of France. Tyrconnel was forced to swear publicly, true or false, that he had never intended to submit to William of Orange but was merely playing for time. He had already decided, however, that before openly declaring against the English settlers and embarking on what must inevitably become a war to the death against the Williamite forces, he must first get rid of Mountjoy who, although until now still staunchly true to King James's cause, would nevertheless not be a party to the oppression of the colonists in any circumstances.

Accordingly Tyrconnel now took the line that King James would not wish his Irish supporters to endanger their cause by striking at an unpropitious moment, but would prefer to wait until the time was ripe. However, as King James in France was ill-informed as to the exact state of things in Ireland, it needed a well-informed and loyal man to go to the court of Louis, where King James was now in residence, and bring him up to date on affairs in Ireland. To perform this task, Tyrconnel chose Mountjoy, and with him he sent Chief Baron Stephen Rice, a Catholic high in the Royal favour. Rice was secretly instructed to tell King James that Mountjoy was a traitor and had only been sent to France to rob the Protestants in Ireland of an effective leader. Rice was also instructed to tell King James that if he came to Ireland quickly enough, with a French force, he might speedily retrieve his fortunes from an Irish base. If James should appear unwilling to come to Ireland and put himself at the head of the native population there, Rice was instructed to seek a private audience with King Louis XIV and to offer Ireland to him, as a province of France.

Rice's instructions accorded with advice which King James had already received from the French. Louis XIV had received King James very nobly, had met him in splendour at Versailles, had housed him in the palace of St Germain-en-Laye, about thirteen kilometres away, and had given him a very generous allowance; but all on the understanding that when the time was ripe, King James would attempt the reconquest of his kingdom, using Ireland as a base if that seemed the best method.

Not many weeks after King William usurped the throne of England, the opportunity came. The time was deemed right for a blow on the flank, and the flank was Ireland. The military decision was Vauban's, but Vauban, the great French military stragetist, did not understand local conditions. The principal problem in Ireland was an almost total lack of the materials of war. There was no shortage of manpower. King Louis' envoys had already written to him enthusiastically about the numbers of young men willing to serve in the army. There would be no great difficulty, they thought, in getting forty or fifty thousand recruits if they should be needed; the only trouble was that there were no arms for them. In training, the recruits rarely handled anything more lethal than staves – some of them iron-tipped but most of them made of wood. On paper, the stand of arms was 20,000; in reality they were in such a condition that only one in twenty could be used, and there was a desperate shortage of artillery.

Tyrconnel was now preparing for the war that seemed inevitable, aided by Hamilton who had given up all thoughts – if he had ever entertained any – of converting Tyrconnel to the Williamite cause, and had openly thrown his hand in on Tyrconnel's side.

The Irish nation was now called to arms – the flag on Dublin Castle carried the slogan: 'Now or Never! Now and Forever!' All over the country Irish peasants abandoned their potato patches and flocked to the colours. They genuinely believed that the tyrants who spoke English and lived in slated houses were about to be swept away for all time and that they were going to get their own lands back. The priests continued, according to reports which reached Dublin Castle, to exhort their congregations to arm themselves against the day when they could fight openly for the Catholic faith, and to regain their old lands. The Irish army under Ormonde had consisted only of eight regiments; it was now increased to forty-eight regiments and the ranks were soon overflowing. But there was a severe shortage of what these days is called 'officer material', and Macaulay refers disparagingly to 'companies commanded by cobblers, tailors and footmen'.

The soldiers were extremely badly paid. The privates received only threepence a day, only half of which was ever paid in the form of currency, and that was usually in arrears.

The other half took the form of a licence to recover the remainder on their own terms. Though four-fifths of the population were Catholic and Irish, more than four-fifths of all the property in Ireland belonged to the English Protestants. It was on the property of the settlers that the swollen Irish army now proceeded to victual itself. The cellars, flocks and herds of the minority were looted by the majority, and whatever was spared by the soldiers was devoured by the camp-followers and by the bands of marauders who soon over-ran the island. Every smith, every cutler, every carpenter was hard at work producing pikes, skeans, and ashen stakes with pointed tips hardened in fire. Macaulay estimated that by February 1689 at least 100,000 Irishmen were in arms, and nearly 50,000 of these were soldiers. The rest were *banditti*, of whom Tyrconnel's government officially disapproved but did nothing to suppress.

The wanton destruction which was achieved by the Irish soldiery and peasants during those few weeks is confirmed by the reports of Protestants who escaped to England, and by letters from the envoys, commissaries and captains of King Louis XIV, who were all agreed that it would take many years to repair the damage which had been wrought within a few short weeks. The chief wealth of Ireland at this period lay in her cattle, fed, as Macaulay puts it, on 'that vast expanse of emerald meadow saturated with the moisture of the Atlantic'. These herds were now ravaged by peasants who regarded meat as the diet of the rich man, and there were stories of carcasses, half raw, half burnt to a cinder, sometimes still alive, being torn to pieces and swallowed without salt, bread or herbs. Sometimes a peasant would kill a cow for its hide, or merely to make himself a pair of brogues; and often a whole herd of sheep was killed and flayed, the fleeces taken away and the bodies left to rot and poison the air.

In Leinster, Munster and Connaught, apart from a few isolated Protestant outposts, it proved quite impossible for the English settlers to resist this onslaught. Fortified houses up and down the country surrendered, their occupants happy to escape with their lives; but many, rather than submit, packed enough for their immediate needs,burned the rest, and set out for Enniskillen or Londonderry.

Meanwhile Mountjoy and Rice had arrived in France, where King James was still living as King Louis' guest in the palace at St Germain-en-Laye. Before he left for France, Mountjoy had submitted his proposals for Londonderry, and Tyrconnel had undertaken to observe them faithfully. They are dated 10 January 1689, and on the same day Mountjoy sent a letter to the garrison at Londonderry telling them that Tyrconnel had agreed to their terms.

On his arrival in France, Mountjoy was immediately thrown into the Bastille. James decided to comply with the invitation extended by Rice — which as we have seen accorded with the advice he had already been given by the French military expert Vauban that the time was ripe for an attack on England via Ireland — and asked Louis for a French army to assist him in his designs. Louis, for a variety of reasons, was reluctant to send a large French army to Ireland at this stage. Principally, he didn't trust King James; the latter had, after all, lost his kingdom without a fight, and had failed altogether to understand the temper of his own English subjects. Consequently, it seemed unlikely to King Louis that he would be successful with the Irish, whose language he didn't even speak, and whose country he had never visited.

But, although he wasn't prepared to risk an army on King James, Louis XIV was nevertheless prepared to supply him with about 400 captains, lieutenants, cadets and gunners, as well as a few top-ranking officers, who, Louis hoped, would be able to achieve the task of re-organizing and disciplining the Irish army. The chief command was given to the Count Conrad de Rosen, a veteran officer. Under him were Maumont, who held the post of Lieutenant-General, and Major-General Pusignan. The expedition also carried about 500,000 crowns in gold, a sum equivalent to about £112,000 then and nearly £1,000,000 today.*

---

*The Bank of England will, reluctantly and guardedly, give an approximate value for the £ at any given period of history. It is based on what they call a 'parcel' made up of a number of staple but extremely varied ingredients — such as how much one would have to pay a man to plough an acre of land, the price of a loaf of bread, the price of a pint of ale, and so on.

On 15 February, James paid a farewell visit to King Louis who remarked — in the nicest possible way — that his dearest wish was that they were to part, never again to meet in this world.

James was accompanied by several of his own subjects who had followed him from England to France, including his son the Duke of Berwick; John Drummond, Earl of Melfort; Cartwright, the Bishop of Chester; and other prominent courtiers. To accompany James and keep an eye on him, Louis chose the Count d'Avaux. One of the Count's tasks was to open lines of communication with the malcontents in the English Parliament and to this end he was given 100,000 crowns.

James arrived at Brest on 5 March, 1689, embarked on a man-of-war called the *St Michael*, and sailed within forty-eight hours. On the afternoon of 12 March he landed at Kinsale, Co. Cork. He was joyously received by the Catholic population and civilly enough by the few Protestants remaining in that area. Perhaps the greetings from the Protestants were not altogether insincere. In Ireland, as in England, there were Protestants whose loyalties were torn between the Divine Right of the hereditary monarch and the Protestant succession; and there was also the fact that King James, although a Catholic, was still an Englishman and King of England, and so might be expected to show more respect for law and order than Tyrconnel and the rabble that was the Irish Army.

King James heard that his cause was prospering in Ireland, and learnt that for all practical purposes the Protestants had been disarmed and defeated in the three southern provinces. In the north there was still some resistance, but before long Hamilton would be marching north with an army, to subdue Enniskillen and Londonderry, and there was little doubt that these towns would soon be crushed.

The 12 and 13 March 1689 were spent at Kinsale and then on 14 March King James left for Cork, where he was received with great pomp and circumstance. Major-General Pusignan, one of the highly experienced French military men who had accompanied the King to Ireland, was despatched to Charlemont to pick up two regiments of horse and to assist

Hamilton in mopping up all resistance in Ulster.

It really was beginning to look as if this was 'Now or Never!' for the Catholic cause in Ireland.

V   *Lundy's treacheries*

In Londonderry, the old Protestant corporation — which took over when Tyrconnel's new Catholic administration fell apart after the closing of the gates of the city — held a meeting on 2 January 1689 to put the defence of the city on a more formal basis. John Campsie was elected Mayor for a year. Cairnes, who should have been in London delivering the letter he had been given for the Irish Society, was at the meeting; his ship had sailed on 11 December but had been driven back by bad weather and he was not able to resume his journey until the weather improved.

Among the decisions reached at this meeting of the corporation was one to send a merchant to Scotland to buy arms with the money which had been freely contributed by the sheriffs, gentlemen, soldiers and merchants of the city and its environs. He succeeded in getting only forty-two barrels of powder. Ten of these were left in Co. Down for the defence of that area, and the remainder were brought into Londonderry and stored in the magazine. Around the same time, a small ship carrying about thirty barrels of powder for the Earl of Antrim's army had to put into Killagh on the coast of Co. Down to shelter from storms. These munitions were seized by the Protestant forces; ten barrels were left in Co. Down, for its defence, and the remainder were added to Londonderry's ever-increasing store. Letters were also despatched at this stage to William of Orange and Queen Mary, now installed in London, asking them for aid.

Apart from arms, Londonderry's prime requirement was food. The inhabitants now made plans to lay in stores for the siege which they felt could not much longer be delayed.

The Mayor saw to it that all the gates were kept locked and that nobody entered without authority. The aldermen and gentry gave generously in supplies as well as money and

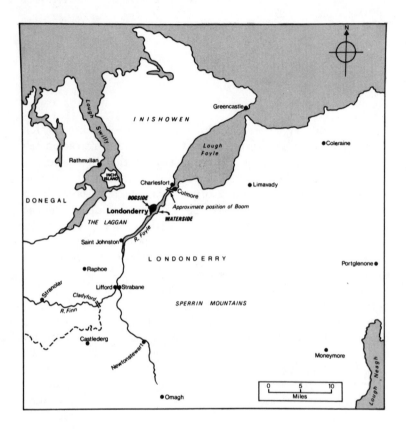

Londonderry and its environs

arms, and many of the merchants contributed stores for the city's defence.

In Enniskillen, the citizens were doing the same thing. By now they had raised a regiment of twelve companies under Gustavus Hamilton, as Governor. Enniskillen, which commanded the principal pass between Connaught and Ulster, was of great strategic importance, and the inhabitants realized this. Between them, Enniskillen and Londonderry, they believed, could foil King James's plans to reduce Ireland and use it as a base for recapturing his Kingdom by invading

Scotland from Ulster, though it must be pointed out that the Ulster Protestants were motivated in their actions far more by fears of another massacre of the Protestants than any desire to foil King James's plans.

Spirits were high both in Enniskillen and Londonderry. The news of what had happened at the Convention of Westminster was received with great rejoicing. William and Mary were proclaimed at Enniskillen with unanimous enthusiasm and as much pageantry as a beleaguered city could afford. This proclamation was also made in Londonderry.

* * *

After he had attended the meeting of the old corporation on 2 January 1689, David Cairnes resumed his voyage to England. The news of the apprentice boys' action and the citizens' stand against Tyrconnel had arrived in England well before him and had been welcomed by the Williamites. Cairnes reached London before the end of January, and he put the case of the Protestants of Ulster — and particularly those in Londonderry — before the Irish Society in London and through the Society he gained an audience with William of Orange. The King directed that measures should be taken at once for forwarding military supplies to the Londonderry garrison.

Captain James Hamilton, later Earl of Abercorn, was immediately sent with arms, ammunition and stores of war, with a commission and instructions for Colonel Lundy as Governor, and a sum of money to be paid to him for the use of the garrison. On his way, Hamilton was to give fifty barrels of powder to any officer holding the King's commission in Co. Down. The supply ship was accompanied by a frigate.

Hamilton was instructed to find out the exact position of the enemy in relation to Londonderry, and to discover how safely the arms and provisions he had with him could be put ashore at or near Londonderry and secured within the town. If this could be done without danger, he was to deliver the commission, money, arms and stores to Lundy or to the

Commander-in-Chief of the city.

There was a great deal of controversy afterwards as to whether Lundy actually took the oaths of fidelity to King William (a matter of more weight then than it would be now), and a number of writers who hold that Lundy was a traitor to the Protestant cause have been at pains to point to all sorts of anomalies in the swearing-in ceremony. Lundy was to take the oath in the presence of the Mayor or the chief civil magistrates of the city, and Hamilton's instructions were that if Lundy failed to take these oaths, or if the approaches to the city proved too dangerous, he was not to land or part with the stores or the commission, but to bring them all safely back to England. These instructions to Hamilton are dated 22 February 1689. The instructions to Lundy, dated the previous day, required him to furnish the garrison with provisions and ammunition for their defence. He was to take measures to improve the defence of the town by cutting dykes, breaking down bridges, and pulling down any houses which might prove prejudicial to the city's defence. To that end, he was supplied with £1,000 (worth over £8,000 today). He was to report on the condition of the place from time to time and to require all officers, civil and military, to take the oath.

Captain Hamilton arrived in Londonderry on Thursday 21 March; his ship the *Deliverance* was accompanied by a frigate, the *Jersey*. Lundy went on board and, according to Mackenzie, instead of taking the oath in public required most of those present to withdraw, thereby suggesting the possibility that he did not sign at all. Mackenzie further states that when asked to take the oath the next day in the city of Londonderry, Lundy refused to do so on the grounds that he had already taken it privately the day before. Oaths are regarded far more seriously in Ireland than they are in England. (De Valera, after all, remained outside the Dail, Ireland's parliament, from 1922 until 1927, because he refused to take an oath of allegiance to the British Crown. In the end he did take it, swearing that it wasn't really an oath and that he wasn't really taking it anyway.) This attachment to oaths in Ireland may in turn explain why there was so much speculation as to whether Lundy had actually taken an oath of allegiance to King William III of England, as he had now become; the controversy raged furiously for a time but there is not much doubt that whether Lundy was or not, the sheriffs, officers and aldermen of Londonderry were all sworn in and the King and Queen again proclaimed.

At a subsequent parliamentary inquiry, which was held to determine whether Lundy had in fact been guilty of treachery, Captain Hamilton said that Lundy was present at the swearing in of the garrison and at the proclamation of the King and Queen on 22 March. He also delivered all the arms and ammunition he had been given, plus the sum of £595 16s 8d which was all that he had succeeded in getting of the £1,000 he had been supposed to pick up at Chester *en route*. The parliamentary committee found that Lundy went on board Hamilton's ship when it arrived on 21 March and that he took the oaths to be true to King William before the commission was delivered to him, in the presence of Colonel Stewart, Captain Corry and other 'persons of substance'.

David Cairnes meanwhile had left London on 12 March for Londonderry. He landed some distance down the lough and on his way met some officers and a great many people leaving Londonderry. On inquiry he found that they had all been given passes by Lundy, who seems at this stage to have been encouraging the principal officers to leave, telling them that the city was untenable. Rumours began to spread that he was planning to hand the city over to the Jacobite army, which was one reason why so many people were leaving; they did not want to be handed over to the enemy.

David Cairnes arrived back in Londonderry on 10 April bringing a letter from the King to Lundy, dated 8 March 1689, directing Cairnes to return to Londonderry and on his arrival there to acquaint the Governor and the magistrates of the King's concern for the city, evidenced by the arms and ammunition he had already sent, and the further preparations he was making not only for the defence of Londonderry but also for the recovery of the whole Kingdom. Cairnes was specifically instructed to discover the present condition of Londonderry as regards men, arms and ammunition and he was to find out whether the countryside around the city could support the much larger force which he was contemplating sending to Ireland and which he hoped would not have to carry provisions from England. This letter, signed by the Earl of Shrewsbury, Secretary of State to William and Mary, stated that the King looked on Ulster as most capable of defending itself against the common enemy, and added that in order to assist it in this effort, two regiments were ready to embark for the province. With them would be sent arms and ammunition, and they would be followed by 'so considerable a body as by the blessing of God may be able to rescue the whole Kingdom and resettle the Protestant religion there.' It was also clear from the letter that the King was looking to Lundy to encourage others in this 'difficult conjuncture', which called upon them for more than ordinary vigour 'to keep out the deluge of Popery and slavery' which threatened them. The King also mentioned that he had recommended the cause of Ireland to the two Houses of Parliament and that he had no doubt that they would show that they espoused Londonderry's interest as their own.

Cairnes delivered this letter and urged Lundy to take effective steps to prevent so many officers and prominent people from leaving the city. Cairnes, who was 44 years of age, was made a Lieutenant-Colonel and stayed on in the city to fight.

A council of war was held that night, at which Cairnes spoke, telling the members of the preparations which were being made in England to send a large force to Ireland and begging them not to desert the city. It was decided at this meeting to choose another 1,000 men to become part of the garrison and join with the soldiers, amateur and professional, who were already defending the walls. The battalions and companies within the city were to have their stations assigned to them, so that they could proceed to these without any fuss or hesitation on any sudden alarm. On the beating of the retreat every night, all the members of the garrison were to repair to their quarters. A gallows was to be erected on one of the bastions upon which all mutinous or treacherous persons were to be executed, to encourage the others. In effect, the city was to be put under martial law. These articles were to be read aloud to every regiment, troop, battalion and company, and any soldier who transgressed them was to be punished. Rations were fixed – very generous rations for a city about to undergo a siege, so generous that one can only assume that the council expected relief to arrive within a matter of a week or two. Every soldier was to receive eight quarts of meal, four pounds of fish and three pounds of meat per week. Soldiers and non-commissioned officers were also to be allowed one quart of small beer per day, 'as soon as the same could be provided', until such time as they came by the money to buy it for themselves.

Captain James Hamilton then proposed the following resolution, which was passed: 'We, the officers hereunto subscribing, pursuant to a resolution taken, and agreed upon at a Council of War at Londonderry held this day, do hereby mutually promise and engage to stand by each other with our forces against the common enemy, and will not leave the kingdom, nor desert the public service, until our affairs are in a settled and secure posture. And if any of us shall do to the contrary, the person leaving the kingdom, or deserting the service without the consent of a Council of War, shall be deemed a coward and disaffected to their Majesties' service and the Protestant interest. Dated the 10th April, 1689.'

This resolution was signed by a number of people other than the officers who were present at the War Council, and it was fixed up in the market place and, along with the articles, was read out to all the soldiers in Londonderry.

Two days later the Mayor John Campsie died suddenly and Alderman Gervais Squire was elected to serve for a year as Mayor in his place.

Still the rumours continued to fly. It was said that a number of leading officers and gentlemen were planning to desert the cause. It was said that if the Protestant forces were driven out of Coleraine they would not be admitted to Londonderry. To scotch these rumours, a Declaration of Unity was drawn up. It was signed by the leading officers and citizens who undertook to oppose the Irish with the utmost force and to receive into the city any Protestants forced to retire there for their safety.

Two days after this declaration was signed, Colonel George Phillips, the former Governor, was sent to England to try to expedite the relief that had been promised by King William.

Tyrconnel's prime objective was now to break down the resistance of the Protestants of Ulster before the promised relief arrived from England. He promoted Richard Hamilton Lieutenant-General and sent him north at the head of 2,500 troops and about the same number of irregulars, with two four-pounders and three twelve-pounder guns. Tyrconnel claimed to be anxious to save from ruin all Protestants who remained quietly in their homes, but although he could make such promises, he could control neither his ill-officered army nor the rabble that always travelled in its wake. Before the path of this army, the settlers burnt their furniture, pulled down their houses, and retreated northwards. A group of them attempted to make a stand at Dromore, Co. Down on 14 March, but they were completely routed. Some fled across the sea to England, Scotland and the Isle of Man, others made their way to Coleraine, Enniskillen and Londonderry.

After wasting several days allowing his troops to pillage the countryside around Dromore, Hamilton marched on Coleraine on 27 March and was driven back, a reverse which caused considerable annoyance and disappointment to King James, who had arrived in Dublin from Cork on 24 March. He was the first English monarch to visit the Irish capital since Richard II about 300 years earlier.

The commander of Coleraine, fearing that his communications with Londonderry might be cut, distributed his forces along the lower Bann and tried to hold on at Moneymore and Magherafelt. Pusignan quickly defeated the Coleraine Protestants at Moneymore, and Hamilton's troops were able to cross the river near Portglenone. The Governor of Coleraine, realizing that his position was rapidly becoming hopeless, abandoned Coleraine and marched for Londonderry on 8 April. The detachments stationed between Moneymore and Portglenone followed him to Londonderry over the mountains.

Meanwhile, the Rev. George Walker, Rector of Donaghmore, a Protestant clergyman and amateur soldier who later became Governor of Derry, had raised a regiment to defend Dungannon. Walker rode into Londonderry to discuss with Lundy some means of keeping open the lines of communication between his forces at Dungannon and the city of Londonderry. Lundy initially agreed to help Walker and sent two troops of dragoons and some experienced men to advise the Dungannon garrison. However, by the middle of March, Lundy had changed his mind and sent orders for the garrison at Dungannon to break up and quit the town. Large quantities of stores had already been laid in for a protracted siege, and as Lundy had made no provision for transferring these to Londonderry, they soon fell into the hands of the Irish army. The garrison of Dungannon was ordered hither and thither by Lundy without apparent reason and eventually joined the Londonderry garrison.

Sligo, another staunch Protestant stronghold commanded by Lord Kingston, was now evacuated on Lundy's orders. Earlier, the Sligo garrison had appealed to Lundy for arms and ammunition, but without any avail. On 20 March, the Sligo garrison received orders to abandon the town and march to Londonderry. There is considerable confusion as to what happened next. Apparently when they arrived at Ballyshannon, Lord Kingston's Sligo Protestants were ordered to remain there. Next an urgent message arrived from Lundy to the effect that Kingston should proceed to Londonderry with 80 of his best horse and 300 foot. Kingston's men, about 1,100 strong, were all against being broken up in this way, and remained at Ballyshannon for the moment, ignoring Lundy's message.

As the Irish army under Hamilton and Pusignan approached ever closer to Londonderry, Lundy began to show alarming signs of inactivity and indecision which were afterwards taken by the fervent Protestants as evidence of his treachery to the Williamite cause. But his vacillations could just as easily be interpreted as the sort of military cock-up that regularly occurs even when men are united against a common enemy without the terrible confusion of loyalties which then existed in Ulster — for, as I have mentioned above, there were many people who were torn between a determination to save and secure the Protestant succession on the one hand, and their belief in the Divine Right of the hereditary monarch on the other.

One Protestant stronghold after another was abandoned: the Protestants believed unnecessarily, though it is doubtful that any of them could have held out for very long as they were widely separated and the lines of communication would have been very easy to sever.

When the Rev. George Walker, who had heard that King James's forces were now moving in strength on Londonderry, rode into the city for the second time within the space of a few weeks to warn Lundy what was happening, Lundy dismissed this warning as a false alarm. On the same day, some of the enemy appeared at the Waterside, on the right bank of the River Foyle, opposite the city. They were in fact Richard Hamilton's troops returning from their attempt on Coleraine. These troops fired a cannon at the New Gate bastion – this was, in fact, the first shot fired in the siege proper – but no damage was done. So inefficient had Lundy's preparations been that the gunner on the bastion had no ammunition ready to return the fire.

Later, the enemy withdrew towards Strabane. There they crossed the River Bann and prepared to ford the Finn, with the object of approaching Londonderry from the Bogside, that is, from the west. Intervening, there were three important passes – Cladyford on the Finn, three miles north of Lifford; Lifford itself; and Long Causey, four miles north of Lifford. If these fords and passes could be held by the Protestants, the Irish Army might be prevented from reaching Londonderry. Lundy had been informed of Hamilton's plan and knew that as the countryside had been 'scorched' by the Protestants before they fled, the enemy could not possibly live off it, but would have to push on to a very fertile area called the Laggan where supplies of food and forage for the horses were still plentiful.

Lundy was now pressured to send troops out to man these passes and prevent the Irish army from breaking through to the fertile lands of the Laggan which, if held, could support the Protestant army until help arrived from England. Under this pressure, Lundy called another council of war and it was decided to march out on 15 April and engage the Irish army at the three passes, Cladyford, Lifford and Long Causey. Lundy himself was to be commander-in-chief in the field.

On Sunday 14 April, David Cairnes warned Lundy that if he did not march at once to secure the passes, it would be too late. The Protestants had already burnt all the corn and forage in the area, so the Irish army could not have survived for long if the passes could only be held. But Lundy stubbornly kept to his original plan of marching out to defend the passes on 15 April.

On that date all males between sixteen and sixty were ordered to meet at the passes, and an estimated 10,000 Protestants turned out. That number includes many men who joined the army on its march.

When the news that King James had arrived in Dublin reached London, there was great alarm and William was criticized for not sending a fleet and an army to Ireland. In the coffee houses, people were gossiping and speculating as to how it had happened that so acute a politician as William could have been fooled by Hamilton and Tyrconnel. In the middle of all this, John Temple, who had recommended Hamilton to the King for the task of persuading Tyrconnel to come over to the Williamite side, took a boat at the Temple stairs, asked to be rowed to Greenwich and, on the way, slipped over the side and drowned himself. He left a suicide note on the seat of the boat. It said: 'My folly in undertaking what I could not execute hath done the King great prejudice which cannot be stopped – No easier way for me than this – May his undertaking prosper – May he have a blessing.' There was no signature but it was not long before the body was recovered and identified. Temple had in fact been forgiven by the King who had already appointed him Secretary at War; Macaulay's theory is that it was 'the cold magnanimity of the master [which] was the very thing which made the remorse of the servant insupportable'.

In Dublin, King James soon found himself caught up in internecine squabbles at Dublin Castle. The trouble was that there was no common ground between English and Irish Jacobitism. The English Jacobite was motivated by a strong enthusiasm for the Stuart family and was prepared to stake everything on securing the Stuart succession. The English and Scottish lords who had accompanied King James from Brest regarded the island on which they now found themselves as merely a stepping stone on the road towards the recovery of England. They felt themselves every bit as much exiles in Dublin as they had been in Paris, a city which they found far more agreeable than Dublin. They had no sympathy with the native population of this remote and barbarous country; on the contrary, they were bound by ties of language and nationality with the settlers whom those peasants were so clearly determined to oust.

The Irish Jacobites, for their part, cared nothing for the Stuart succession and were against all foreign sovereigns. Their fixed purpose was to break for all time the 'foreign yoke', to exterminate the English settlers or force them to clear out to England, to sweep away the Protestant Church and to restore all Irish lands to their former owners. If these ends could be achieved by means of a temporary liaison with King James, then they were prepared to fight under him, but they didn't really care if he never saw Whitehall again. Their real aim was to sever Ireland from England, with or without James's help, and many of them held the view that, if necessary, Ireland should become a separate Catholic state under the protection of France.

In the meantime the Count d'Avaux and the French faction at Dublin Castle viewed the question from yet another point of view. Their object was neither the restoration of King James nor the emanicipation of Ireland, but the enlargement of Louis XIV's empire. Assuming, as they secretly did, that King William could not be dislodged from the English throne, they reckoned that the most beneficial arrangement would be that Ireland should be severed from the English crown, purged of all English colonists and settlers, reunited with the Church of Rome, and put under French protection, to become, in everything but name, a province of France. Ireland would thus be able to furnish the French army with an endless supply of recruits and the French navy with a series of fine harbours commanding the western outlets of the British mainland. So the French faction favoured the Irish cause, but for their own reasons.

The first practical question to be settled was whether King James should remain in Dublin or put himself at the head of the army before Londonderry. The Irish were anxious that he should remain in Dublin, because if he did so, he could hardly refrain from giving his assent to the many bills which they were busy preparing to present to Parliament. Some of these measures James was reluctant to accept because they would have meant plundering and attainting Protestant gentlemen who, although Protestants, were nevertheless his own fellow-countrymen. The English Jacobites wanted him to go to Londonderry because if it fell, as they believed it would, within a few days, King James would be within a short voyage of Scotland, where supposedly his friends were numerous and where he could form the nucleus of an army and march on London.

In the event, James elected to go north, against the express advice of Tyrconnel, whom he had just created a Duke. The Count d'Avaux decided to go with James to keep an eye on things, and the royal party set out on 13 April. It was a dreadful journey, through a wasteland deserted by the population and laid waste by bands of robbers. A French officer described it as 'like travelling through the deserts of Arabia'. Whatever valuable effects the colonists had been able to remove were now housed at Londonderry or Enniskillen. Everything else had been destroyed by them before they left, or plundered by the banditti. The ambassador Avaux was put one night into a miserable taproom full of soldiers smoking, another night in a dismantled house without windows or shutters to keep out the rain. At Charlemont, Macaulay says, 'a bag of oatmeal was with great difficulty, and as a matter of favour, procured for the French legation. There was no wheaten bread except at the table of the King, who had brought a little flour from Dublin, and to whom Avaux had lent a servant who knew how to bake. Everybody else, however high in rank, ate horsecorn and drank water or detestable beer, made with oats instead of barley, and flavoured with some nameless herb as a substitute for hops.'

It was while he was on his way to Charlemont that King James heard that the Protestants had abandoned Coleraine and that Pusignan had marched to get between the Protestants of Coleraine and Londonderry and had failed. He also heard that the Protestants had been carrying out a 'scorched earth' policy to prevent Hamilton's troops from getting their supplies from the land. Apart from a small number of troops who might be able to cross by the ferry from the Waterside, the bulk of the Irish army would have to go to Strabane and Lifford to get to the Laggan, that fertile area around Raphoe on which it might be possible for an army to subsist, and from which an attack on Londonderry could be made from the Bogside. James gave orders for Hamilton and Pusignan to march towards Strabane, the former by way of Omagh, the latter via Derry and Tyrone.

James then continued on towards Omagh on 14 April. It poured with rain and the travellers had to pass through several fords where the water was breast-high. In forty miles Avaux counted only three miserable cabins. Everything else was rock, bog and moorland. When they reached Omagh they found it in ruins. Pusignan's foot soldiers had already been there and had left under the command of Colonel Ramsey, while Pusignan himself had gone on in advance of them to Newtownstewart, which the Protestants had now abandoned along with Omagh.

It was 15 April, and Pusignan advanced to Cladyford where the Protestant army from Londonderry was assembling. When it was reported to James that the Protestants were in great strength on the other side of the Finn at Cladyford, he sent Rosen, Maumont and Lery before him with the rest of the troops that were available, hoping that they might be able to force a passage at Lifford. Hamilton, Berwick and Pusignan had in the meantime joined their troops at Strabane and forced the passage at Cladyford with a mere handful of men 'in sight of five or six thousand of the enemy that were on the other side to oppose them', as King James himself put it.

According to James, Rosen, not finding the others at Strabane when he arrived there, went forward to view the passage of the river from Strabane to Lifford with two troops of horse and one of dragoons, and although the Protestant army on the other side was ten times as numerous managed to force a passage. They crossed the river, the footsoldiers clinging on to the tails and manes of the horses as they swam across. This action so frightened the Protestant troops from

Londonderry that they fled three or four miles away from the scene. James, quite wrongly, interpreted this hasty withdrawal – which in modern parlance was simply a shambles – as a sign that the Protestants were reserving their principal strength for the ultimate defence of Londonderry.

Reports of this engagement are so confused that it is only possible to piece together a vague account of it from the various reports made by the protagonists. Berwick, for example, says that he had received orders to go north to serve under Hamilton, and when he joined Hamilton they advanced on Coleraine which they found had already been abandoned by the Protestants. From there they marched to Cladyford where they found about 10,000 Protestants assembled to dispute the passage. According to his account, the Jacobites had no more than 350 foot and 600 horse. There was no ford and the bridge was broken, but Hamilton ordered his men to swim for it, and the Jacobites managed to cross with the loss of only one officer and two privates drowned. The infantry contrived a bridge with planks, crossed over and began to fire on the main body of Protestants who, instead of advancing to attack the Jacobites as they came out of the water, dripping wet and unable to use their firearms, took fright. The Jacobites claimed to have killed about 400 of the Protestant infantry on the spot, but could not catch up with their cavalry. It was during this action that Rosen arrived, saw the enemy ranged on the other side of the river, and had his men swim the river in the same way. The Jacobite army was amazed at the lack of initiative shown by the defenders of Londonderry. As the Jacobites emerged from the water, half-drowned, the horse towing the infantry by mane and tail after them, with scarcely a dry shot left, they were extremely vulnerable. Whether the fault lay with the spirit of the Protestant forces or with Lundy's direction of them it is impossible to say. Mackenzie, who served in Londonderry throughout the siege and was one of Lundy's severest critics, says: 'Lundy was so far from putting the Protestants in any posture to oppose them, that upon their entering the ford, he gave orders to all thereabouts to flee to Derry, himself leading the way.'

Walker had taken the post at Long Causey but having

waited too long for orders which never came, he felt himself
and his troops to be in danger and withdrew. Captain Thomas
Ash, another of Lundy's critics – he also served in the siege
and published an account of it – argued that if Lundy had
marched his men out on Sunday 14th, as he had been urged to
do, the enemy 'had probably not all so easily have gotten
over', although even on Monday 15th the Londonderry
Protestants allowed the Jacobite army to cross the river when
they outnumbered them by five to one. Ash denounced
Lundy's conduct as inexcusable, 'both in abandoning so
many passes, and those easily defensible by a few men, if
they had been supplied with ammunition, or constantly
relieved, and never so much as attempting to draw the forces
into a body when they were in the field above 10,000 men
who, whatever he pretended to the contrary, wanted more
care and resolution in their leader than courage in themselves.'

Walker says that the soldiers were supplied with only three
charges of powder per man. There seems to be little doubt
that Lundy panicked. There are reports of him leaving parties
of up to 200 Protestants cut off, and fleeing, shouting: 'You
are all cut off. Shift for yourselves.' There are reports, too,
that when the retreating army arrived, at Lundy's instruction,
back in Londonderry, it found Lundy already safely inside
and the gates locked against it, so that some 8,000 men had
to spend the night outside, exposed to the Irish army and the
rabble which accompanied it. Some of them were in fact
killed at Inishowen, just outside the city gates.

Evidence at the subsequent parliamentary inquiry
indicated that Lundy himself was one of the first to flee,
bidding his men to shift for themselves and saying that all
was lost. Colonel Chichester met Lundy running away from
the pass, and told him that he should stay with his men and
give them some orders. Lundy replied that Londonderry was
his post, and that that was where he was going. It also seems
to be generally agreed that as soon as he got there, Lundy let
in a few men, as he felt inclined, and then locked the
remainder of his own troops outside the city walls, to fend
for themselves as best they could.

On the question of the failure to hold the passes, it appears

that the men had not sufficient powder to fight effectively
and had never received any positive orders. Scarcely three
shots were fired, reported Lord Blaney of Armagh, 'before all
were routed'. Lundy's defence was that the men would not
stand at the pass but ran away at the first sight of the
Jacobite army and that he merely fled along with the rest,
which may well be true.

Lundy later justified his action in closing the gates of
Londonderry against his own comrades by saying that he was
afraid that if he did not do so, the rabble would get in and
make serious inroads into their scant provisions. Walker says
that Lundy and several of the 'quality' were at the head of
those retreating to Londonderry, and asserts that he himself
was locked outside the gates all night; indeed it was with
great difficulty and after some violence with the sentry that
he managed to get in the next day. Walker in fact goes so far
as to suggest that when he left Londonderry, Mountjoy gave
Lundy secret instructions to accept whatever directions he
might receive from Paris. He gives no justification for this
suggestion other than the theory that Mountjoy was trying to
insinuate himself into King James's favour by promising to
make Lundy an instrument for the breaking of the Protestant
power in Ireland. On Mountjoy's character and past performance this seems unlikely.

Whatever his motives, when eventually a formidable Irish
army marched on Londonderry, Lundy stayed resolutely
within the walls of the city and refused to sally out and
attack the Irish army, despite many attempts to make him
do so. As we have seen, he allowed the counties of Down and
Armagh to be over-run, he persuaded Lord Kingston to
abandon Sligo, he failed to supply Enniskillen and
Ballyshannon with the ammunition they so badly needed and
he could not be urged to get forage into Londonderry,
despite the fact that the surrounding countryside offered vast
quantities of hay and oats. Furthermore, he continued to give
passes to any who asked for them, and seemed for a time at
any rate to be trying to convince the ablest and most resolute
men that there was no chance of defending Londonderry and
that their best course would be to get out while the going was
good.

According to some reports, when the enemy neared Londonderry Lundy initially went out with some 7,000 men, but as soon as the Irish army advanced again, he lost his nerve and shouted: 'Gentlemen, I see you will not fight', although his men were willing and eager to fight. Once again he retreated into the city and had the gates locked in the face of his comrades who were left outside the walls, at the mercy of the Irish army.

As the Irish army continued its victorious drive towards Londonderry, Protestant forces and refugees kept crowding into the city; for despite Lundy's instructions, the gates were soon opened again. These refugees have been described, in C.D. Milligan's *History of the Siege of Londonderry,* as 'an unarmed people flying before a powerful army grown insolent by uninterrupted success, and seeking shelter in a city which could not contain one hundredth part of those who retreated to it, and for many there was nothing to be done to escape sudden destruction or lingering death by famine but to fly over the sea and preserve life, which was all that was left to them.' By now some 30,000 souls were crowded behind the city walls, including many troops from the neighbouring Protestant strongholds such as Lord Mountjoy's dragoons raised in Newtownards, Lieutenant Colonel Sir George Maxwell's regiment from Killyleagh, and Lord Blaney's regiment from Armagh.

During the heat of the battle for the passes, Lundy had ordered Lord Kingston and his Sligo men to proceed towards Londonderry to see how matters stood there. When they reached Stranorlar, they met some Protestant troops running away from Cladyford. These said that Lundy and his forces had retreated to Londonderry and that the Irish were at Raphoe, so that Kingston's path to the city was barred. Lord Kingston and his men returned to Ballyshannon, and after giving instructions for the horse to secure themselves in Enniskillen and the foot at Ballyshannon, Kingston himself took a ship from Killybegs to Scotland to try to secure some relief from England. In the meantime, the Irish forces had now over-run Sligo and the neighbouring countryside.

Tyrconnel had given orders to Lundy to send to Dublin the four companies of Mountjoy's regiment which had not been admitted to Londonderry as well as the two companies which had. These instructions were ignored and instead the other four companies, which by now had been purged of Catholics, were admitted to the city. Joint guards were posted consisting of detachments from the six companies of Mountjoy's regiment and the six companies from the city.

But this arrangement didn't work. Lundy refused ammunition to the city companies, cancelled the arrangement under which joint guards were to be mounted and tried to bring the command of the city guard entirely under his own officers.

It was plain that an open break between Lundy and the townspeople of Londonderry could not now be long delayed.

VI *King James arrives at Londonderry*

King James arrived in Omagh on 14 April. News reached him there of three or four thousand Protestants on the march near Strabane and thirteen English ships, including four warships, off Londonderry. This information set him off on a whole train of baffling vacillations, decisions and redecisions. At first, he sent for the Count d'Avaux and announced that he was returning to Dublin at once. Avaux agreed with this decision and said that it would be quite enough to send Rosen and the other generals to assist the Irish army to invest the city. James accordingly ordered them to set off for Londonderry and started to make his own preparations for a return to Dublin.

He was next informed that an officer of the dragoons, who was escorting some barrels of powder, had fallen in with the enemy which was now in strength around Omagh. The Count d'Avaux advised that infantry should be posted to guard the bridge and a cavalry patrol sent out to see whether this information was accurate. This was done, but James didn't bother to wait for the cavalry patrol to return; instead he fled the town, only to discover that the officer in question had indeed given a false alarm, and that the soldiers he had mistaken for the enemy were in fact Irish soldiers marching to join King James. James now changed his mind again, and on hearing of the success of Pusignan and Hamilton at Cladyford, decided to follow Rosen towards Londonderry. Avaux and Melfort – who had been appointed Secretary of State for Ireland when James landed in Kinsale – explained to him that this success was a very slight one and should in no way influence his decision to return to Dublin, and so persuaded him to go with them to Charlemont, which was on the way to Dublin.

On 15 April, James heard more details of Hamilton's

successes at the Finn and Lifford and again heard that there were English ships in Lough Foyle. Believing that the Protestants were staking all on the defence of Londonderry he now thought he would go to Dublin and provide whatever was necessary for the conduct of the siege in the way of men and materials. At this juncture, he seems to have decided to give the honour of accepting the surrender to Rosen; though to be cynical, it is possible that with the arrival of the British ships in the Foyle, furnished with supplies of men and arms and ammunition, it may have occurred to him that Londonderry might not surrender so readily after all, in which case it might be more politic if the King himself were not present at the *débâcle*.

On 16 April, the Count d'Avaux joined the King at Charlemont. James had now definitely made up his mind to leave the command to Rosen, Maumont, Hamilton, Berwick, Lery and the others, and he was all set to return to Dublin when word reached him that there was such a general dismay among the Protestants over their defeat at Cladyford that Londonderry was on the point of surrendering without resistance. On the morning of 17 April, the Duke of Berwick wrote to the King to the effect that Rosen, Maumont and Lery had just joined Hamilton and Pusignan, that he didn't believe thirteen English ships had come into the Foyle and that the generals were now all of the opinion that if James would but show himself before the gates of Londonderry, the city would surrender.

On the same day, Berwick sent another express to James to the effect that 'the rebels of Londonderry' had sent to treat with Hamilton. Berwick added that it was still the general opinion that the town would surrender on the appearance of the King at the city walls.

James consulted the Count d'Avaux who repeated his very cogent argument: that if Londonderry did not attempt to defend itself, then it would be taken before the King had time to show himself before the gates; on the other hand, if the city resisted, the King might well have to retrace his footsteps with a certain loss of prestige. He advanced another very valid argument for the King not showing himself before Londonderry at this stage. If the King appeared with a small army, which was all he had, the besieged would know exactly what forces he had at his disposal; on the other hand, if he refrained from appearing, they might assume that the King himself was waiting in the rearguard with a very formidable army. Avaux also threw in the argument that the honour of being there to take the surrender of Londonderry would not equal the vexation he would suffer if the city refused to surrender.

But all Avaux's arguments were useless. James now changed his mind again, and decided to appear before Londonderry at the head of his army, among other reasons to disabuse the rebels there of a rumour that was current that the king had died at Brest. Hilaire Belloc in his history, *James the Second,* advances three excuses for this grave error in judgement: first, that no English authority since the Lancastrian usurpation of the English throne in the Middle Ages had ever attempted to understand Irish conditions; second, that he had had the recent experience of the enthusiasm for his claims in the south, in Dublin, where a considerable body of Protestants had apparently accepted him readily enough; and third, that the man in command at Londonderry, Lundy, was widely believed to be on the point of yielding.

James rode off that day to Newtownstewart, rested for three or four hours in his clothes, and was off again the next day to Strabane. There he received a report from Rosen that the inhabitants of the town had indicated their willingness to capitulate, and in order to induce them to do so more readily, Rosen urged that James should show himself immediately before the city with his whole army. Rosen further informed the King that there were English ships in the Foyle with reinforcements and supplies for the city.

James had expected to find the army at Strabane but they were already on their way to Londonderry, so he did not stop but carried on and soon overtook the foot, under Pusignan and Ramsey, two miles beyond Lifford. They told King James that Rosen was up ahead with some horse and dragoons, so James continued on, after having reviewed the foot from horseback. Rosen had left Strabane four hours before James, having sent part of his horse ahead the previous day to Raphoe, partly because there was plenty of forage in that area, and partly in the hope that they might drive any Protestants still in the area further into Inishowen. These horse and dragoons, commanded by Hamilton and Berwick, had instructions to rejoin Rosen within sight of Londonderry.

James caught up with Rosen within a few miles of Londonderry. He put himself at the head of the army and proceeded towards the town, stopping on a hill just beyond cannon-shot of it.

When the foot arrived, Rosen posted them all round the town. James then prepared to summon the city but Rosen advised him to wait until the troops were brought up in full strength. As the footsoldiers were being posted by Rosen around the city, James, still keeping well outside cannon range, sent a trumpet – that is, a trumpeter, plus an envoy – to summon it. The trumpet returned with the message that the citizens would send their reply in an hour's time, and meanwhile King James's troops were to approach no closer. Rosen paid no attention to this but continued to post his men about the city.

The answer that came from the garrison in less than an hour's time was a fusillade of cannon and musket shot from the city walls, and some of the King's soldiers were killed. There seems to have been some indecision in the city because, according to King James's own account of the affair, others came out of the city and assured the King that these shots came only from the rabble who, being drunk, had seized the cannon and had fired it without any authority from the officers; and furthermore, that the 'people of a better sort' were disposed to surrender and were doing all they could to try to persuade the common people to do the same.

The version of the Londonderry citizens reflects this indecision. A message was sent to King James, who was thought to be at St Johnston. He had not in fact arrived there, though Hamilton had. This message indicated the city's willingness to surrender on an understanding that King James would grant a general pardon and order restitution of all that had been plundered from the Protestants in Londonderry.

Some of the gentlemen in Londonderry were influenced by these considerations to subscribe, but others not only refused, but began to suspect Governor Lundy of foul play. Some even went so far as to threaten to hang the Governor and his council.

On the same day the Rev. Whitelow, Minister of Raphoe, came to Londonderry from Hamilton to propose a treaty for the surrender of the town. Another council of war was held. Lundy told this council that the town could not hold out, but must surrender. The council then sent Archdeacon Hamilton, Captain Charles Kinaston and Captain Francis Nevill to Hamilton to seek terms. They were given one article to present to the garrison. It was signed by Hamilton and Rosen and required the surrender of the city with all serviceable horses and arms, and guaranteed that the garrison could live peaceably. An answer was required by noon the next day, 18 April, until which time it was agreed that the Irish army would not come within a certain distance of the town – the actual distance differs in various accounts between two and a half and five miles.

When this deputation returned on the night of 17 April, feelings in the city were running so high that they were refused admittance. Later Archdeacon Hamilton and Captain Kinaston managed to get in, but Captain Whitney, who was in charge of the gate, denied Captain Nevill entrance and he had to spend the whole night outside the walls.

In spite of the agreement that the Jacobite army would remain a certain distance from the walls until the time stipulated in the article had expired, James arrived with his colours flying on the morning of 18 April. He came to the strand at the south end of the city near the Bishop's Gate at about 10 a.m. The war council had given instructions that there was to be no firing until King James had made his demands known, but the garrison were by now so suspicious of the war council that they paid no attention to these orders, and reckoning that Hamilton had broken his word by allowing the King approach so close before noon on 18 April, they opened fire on the Irish army and killed some of them, including members of King James's own personal bodyguard.

Accompanying the shots from the ramparts were cries of 'No Surrender!' James, who had certainly been assured by his senior officers that the mere sight of His Majesty and his army would cause the immediate capitulation of the city and also possibly – though this was by no means so certain – had been assured by traitors within the city that it would be immediately delivered up to him, was greatly shocked at the reception he received and quickly withdrew beyond the point of danger. He remained on horseback all day in the rain, while the men on Londonderry's ramparts, ignoring the war council, continued to fire at his retreating troops.

Lundy hurriedly covened another meeting of his war council which decided to send an apology to King James explaining what had happened and pointing out that the mob had fired upon his army without any express authority. There is still some confusion as to who actually carried this message to James; as there was still some doubt as to whether the King was actually present, a Captain White, who had often seen him before, was, according to Mackenzie, sent with Archdeacon Hamilton to resolve all doubts on the matter, and this seems likely. Mackenzie says that White returned with the news that the King was indeed there in person, while Archdeacon Hamilton sought protection and remained with the Jacobites.

A few hours earlier, the Earl of Abercorn had arrived with a parley – that is to say, a party empowered to negotiate – from King James for the surrender of the city, offering the inmates their lives, estates, freedom of religion and a free pardon for all their past offences. But by now the people were past any form of parley and refused to surrender on any conditions whatsoever.

Rosen was for marching his army right under the walls to frighten the garrison into submission. Hamilton was against this because he felt that if the citizens of Londonderry saw how ill-equipped the Irish army was, in regard especially to mortars and artillery, it would merely make them more obstinate in their determination to resist.

In this, Hamilton was right. The paucity of artillery in the Irish army seems to have been extreme. In their first march northwards, something like 5,000 foot and 800 or 900 horse had been accompanied by exactly two guns. Under the walls of Londonderry, as the siege began, there were about 10,000 men but only three field pieces, two small mortars and two siege guns, firing shot of not more than twelve pounds apiece – and these to attack walls twenty-four feet high and eight or nine feet thick, and defended by thirty pieces of ordnance.

Of the muskets, the proportion which could be safely used was negligible. 'Out of every ten muskets,' wrote Hamilton, 'one might be counted upon to shoot.' In a letter to Louis XIV's war minister, the French envoy refers to a colonel of the regiment during the siege who reported that in all his regiment there were only seven muskets; the other troops had 'little sticks three feet long' and a few, he added, had pikes but without any iron on them. He goes on to say that there was no organization of hospitals, no medicines or provisions. In his life of King James II, Belloc gives an instance where, in the absence of firearms, an attempt was made to rush up, over the vile roads and in abominable weather, a supply of sabres for the cavalry. They arrived without belts or sheaths so that the unfortunate soldiers had to carry their sabres drawn in their hands, simply because there was nowhere else to put them.

The shortage of firearms produced some Gilbertian situations. When a captain in O'Neill's regiment died, twenty-five of his dragoons immediately deserted, taking their horse with them, and the remainder of the Captain's command argued that they did not need to serve any further, as they had engaged themselves personally to their officer and to nobody else. This was, of course, standard practice in Europe at this period. The mutineers were tried by court martial and condemned to draw lots so that one of them might be executed as an example to the others. This was done but when the unlucky man had drawn his lot there was not a firearm in the whole command which would go off, and they had to beg one off another unit, Lord Mayo's, before they could despatch the victim. And these men were dragoons – mounted infantry specially detailed for fighting on foot with firearms.

The truth, Belloc sums up, is that the expedition could not

conceivably succeed against the force which an organized English government would sooner or later send against it, nor could it even succeed against the small, walled town of Londonderry, with which it first had to deal.

So Hamilton was probably right in arguing that the inadequacies of the Irish army should have been kept out of sight of the defenders of Londonderry. However, in the event, Rosen had his way. Not that it would have made much difference. At this moment, the citizens of Londonderry were determined not to surrender in any circumstances. By now the 'quality' had thrown in their lot with the rabble and the city was, on the whole, united.

James, using the official excuse of bad weather, drew off his troops to the nearest town to await cannon and various other necessities of a full-scale siege or blockade which were on the way from Dublin. He retired to St Johnston, where he made his headquarters at Monglevin Castle.

On 19 April, the King was installed at St Johnston and he sent a letter signed by Melfort, his Secretary of State for Ireland, to the townsfolk of Londonderry. This letter was delivered by the Earl of Abercorn and read as follows:

JAMES REX

> Whereas we have given leave to such as are assembled in our City of Derry, to send such of their number as they shall think fit, not exceeding twenty, to whom we are pleased to give our Royal Pass and safe conduct to come to our quarters, and return again in safety, provided that they come within twelve hours from the date of these presents, in company with my Lord Abercorn, who is hereby ordered to conduct them to us with all civility and safety, and in the same manner to reconduct them in safety again. We do therefore expressly command all our General Officers, and all others our officers and soldiers and subjects whatsoever, to take notice of this our Royal Pass and safe conduct, as they shall answer the contrary to their utmost peril. We will explain this our Royal Will in a most extensive and honourable manner for the same persons, we being resolved on our part to observe the same most punctually —
> Given at our quarters at St. Johnston, 14th day of April, 1689,

at four o'clock in the afternoon, in the fifth year of our Reign.
By his Majesty's command,
Melfort.

The answer was returned that whether James were there or
not, the city would not surrender. The date of the letter was
19 April, one day after the King arrived in St Johnston, and
the Earl of Abercorn was not admitted with this letter,
although he did deliver it with threats that the inhabitants, if
they did not immediately comply with the King's wishes,
would be attacked with all manner of bombs, fireworks, and
so on.

A number of Protestants laid down their arms following
this message and went to St Johnston where the King gave
them protection, as he had promised.

Lundy's council of war now received the following letter
from Hamilton:

Gentlemen,
Here is your King that resolves to perform all Conditions you
can desire; and that, too, under his Hand and Seal, before
twenty witnesses of your own. You shall have the honour of
delivering the Keys of your City to his Royal hands, shall be
treated as Favourites, and Finishers of this difficult siege, and
the intire reduction of Ireland, and faithful subjects of this
Kingdom. Whether it is two to one whether you are able to
withstand this dreadful Army, and defend your city from utter
Ruin and Destruction. Yet if so wonderful a Deliverance
should attend you, your Rewards notwithstanding will be
uncertain and future interest will always be prized beyond past
merit; eaten bread is commonly forgotten and former services
are too often swallowed up in oblivion, especially if there be
no future expectation from those that performed them. So
that all assurances you depend on will vanish into the air, and
the result of all your hardships, will be only the repetition of
this miserable proverb, We have Our Labour for our pains; but
on the contrary, if you submit to your lawful King, and join
with us, all the lands of the Absentees and all such forfeiting
persons, shall be the purchase of your submission and the
reward of your loyalty to your rightful soverign; and besides
your own estates (which are now forfeited) shall be confirmed
to you, by an Act of Parliament now sitting, of which you

yourselves shall have the wording; and such of you as are strong and stout, shall serve with us in Scotland and in England where Thousands of both Nations are ready to receive us and join us (all waiting on the success of this bloody siege) with Several Thousands of the French. The Commissioned Officers shall be continued in the same Posts at least, if not advanced to a better, and them we shall esteem as Hostages for their Families, which will make us dependent upon them the more; and when it shall please God to give us victory in England, which in a few months we hope to accomplish, that even there you shall come in as Sharers in the forfeited lands. And as for Scotland, Duke Gordon is now in possession of the Castle of Edinburgh for the King, Dundee is in arms and all the King's Friends are ready to receive him. But if you continue obstinate, your Ruin seems inevitable, by withstanding an Army so well-disciplined and so powerful; which resolves, if you continue obstinate, to give no Quarter to Man, Woman or Child. Whence once our Cannon and Mortars have rent the Walls in pieces, and the Town is taken by Storm, then thousands of your Wives and Children shall fall upon their knees, and with repeated Sighs and Groans implore our pity, we shall doubtless be inexorable, and all their cries will be drown'd in the loud Acclamations of our victorious Army, which will then be deaf and merciless. And therefore, before it is too late, consider and resolve that Mercy, which your King is now willing to grant, before you find it will be too late, and that it will be out of his power to preserve them from the Rage and Slaughter of an enraged Army, whose Fury cannot be withheld by His Majesty, much less by,

Gentlemen,
Your most humble servant,
Richard Hamilton.

A council considered this letter and decided to send twenty men to go to James and arrange a capitulation. When the twenty commissioners had finally been chosen, the multitude on the walls and at the gates refused to let them leave the city and threatened that if anybody went out of the city for the purpose of surrendering it, they would be treated as betrayers of the Crown, the Protestant religion and King William's cause.

Instead, the garrison sent this answer to the King:

Sir,

The Cause we have undertaken, we design for ever to maintain; and question not, but that powerful Providence which has hitherto been our Guardian, will finish the Protection of us, against all your Attempts, and give a happy issue to our Arms. We must let you know that King William is as capable of rewarding our Loyalty as King James; and that an English Parliament can be just as bountiful to our Courage and Sufferings as an Irish one; and that in time we question not but your Lands will be forfeited rather than ours and confiscated into our Possession, as a recompense for this Signal Service to the Crown of England, and for this inexpressible Toil and Labour, Expence of Blood and Treasure, pursuant to their Sacred Majesties' Declaration to that purpose; a true Copy whereof we herewith send you, to convince you how little we dread your Menaces.

We remain, etc.,

Before this letter was delivered, a trumpet came to the walls on the evening of 19 April, inquiring why the town had not sent out twenty commissioners to treat, according to the proposals in Hamilton's letter.

On receiving the letter from the garrison, James sent a *carte blanche* signed by himself and inviting the garrison to insert their own terms for surrender, but when this elicited no reply he returned with Rosen and Lery, very mortified, leaving Maumont, Berwick and Pusignan to assist Hamilton to besiege the city.

With ill-concealed satisfaction, the Count d'Avaux wrote to Louis XIV: 'He offered to pardon all those who surrendered, but it was all in vain. They told him on the last occasion not to send again as the trumpeter would be fired on.'

VII   *The end of Lundy*

It is now time to clear up the question of the English ships rumoured to be at the mouth of Lough Foyle. On 15 April, eleven ships carrying two regiments of Williamite forces, plus a supply of arms and ammunition, anchored in the bay.

Colonel John Cunningham was in charge of this first relief expedition, with Colonel Solomon Richards as his second-in-command. Cunningham's initial orders are dated 12 March 1689. The regiments were to disembark at Londonderry, together with arms and stores for the city. Matthew Anderton, a collector of taxes, was authorized to give Cunningham about £2,000 (worth over £16,000 today) for the subsistence of the regiments and the relief of Londonderry.

On his arrival, Cunningham was to find out whether the city was still in the hands of the Protestants and whether he could safely put two regiments ashore and see that they were quartered comfortably in the Londonderry district. During his stay he was to follow Governor Lundy's instructions to the letter, and he was to assure the Governor and the inhabitants of Londonderry that more men, arms and ammunition – as well as more money – would shortly be sent from England for their relief. In the meantime, Cunningham was to entertain as good a correspondence with the Governor as he found necessary for the King's service and was to make the best defence he could against all persons who attempted to besiege the town or annoy the Protestants in it in any way whatsoever.

While Cunningham was to endeavour by all prudent means to get the regiments into Londonderry, he was not to expose them to any undue hazard in doing so, and if he found it difficult to land them safely at or near Londonderry, he was to attempt a landing at Carrickfergus or Strangford Lough.

And if he found it impossible to land them safely anywhere, he was to bring them back with him to Liverpool. On arrival in Londonderry he was to pay £500 to Lundy as a royal bounty 'in part of the reward we intend him for his faithful services'. The remainder of the money Cunningham had picked up from the tax collector in Chester was to go toward the cost of securing the garrison or whatever place that Cunningham decided to put the regiments ashore.

It had originally been intended to send four regiments to Ireland under Major-General Percy Kirke, but, in the event, only two regiments, Cunningham's own, the 9th, and Colonel Richards's, the 17th, were conveniently situated in Liverpool. They sailed on 10 April, under escort of the frigate, *Swallow*. They had previously set sail on 3 April, but had been driven back by bad weather.

Captain Thomas Ash records their arrival in Londonderry on 15 April (Macaulay puts the date at 14 April) and says that there were eleven ships in all and 1,600 men. The fleet anchored off Culmore fort to wait for a suitable tide before continuing up to Londonderry.

Cunningham wrote three letters on the day of his arrival in Lough Foyle; they were all addressed to Governor Lundy. The first was written from Greencastle at about 10 a.m. and informed Lundy of his arrival and asked for his instructions with regard to the two regiments on board.

This, it will be remembered, was the day of the attempted defence of the fords at Clady, Lifford and Long Causey and when, by 2 p.m., Cunningham, who knew about the garrison's actions, received no reply, he sent a second letter to Lundy, from the *Swallow*, near Redcastle. In this second letter, he stated that he had learnt that Lundy had taken the field to fight the enemy at the passes on the Finn and informed him that he had two regiments on board which could join in the fight in two days at the latest; Cunningham added that he thought these experienced troops would be of considerable advantage to Lundy's 'raw men', as he believed them to be.

Cunningham, who had obviously studied the terrain, expressed the opinion that Lundy had only to hold the passes at the fords on the Finn until he joined them, and afterwards, if they had to fight a pitched battle, Lundy would be in a far stronger position with his (Cunningham's) experienced troops at his side. He added that Their Majesties had left the final decision in all matters to Lundy, and said that he was prepared to obey Lundy's instructions.

When by 9 p.m. he had received no answer to this second letter, he sent a third from the fort at Culmore, requesting orders from Lundy and some advice as to the best means of putting ashore the two regiments he had on board.

On his way to Londonderry, carrying Cunningham's third letter, the messenger met another messenger carrying Lundy's replies to Cunningham's earlier letters, which Lundy had received on his return to Londonderry after the retreat from Cladyford. In his replies to Cunningham's letters, Lundy said that things were in a great state of confusion in Londonderry and were much worse than Cunningham could imagine. He ordered Cunningham to leave the fleet at anchor in the Foyle estuary, and to come the following morning to the city with Colonel Richards and whatever other officers he saw fit to include, to attend a council of war and to hear a further account of the current state of the Londonderry garrison.

On the morning of 16 April, Cunningham and Richards with several of their officers, plus one officer of the fleet, went to Londonderry and there met Lundy and a number of officers from the Londonderry garrison. A council of war was held. It was complained, by Walker and others, that the composition of this council of war included far too many gentlemen — such as Cunningham and Richards and their officers, and the master of the *Swallow* — completely unacquainted with the temper of the town and the attitudes of its inhabitants. Lundy refused to admit officers who had been present at earlier councils of war, such as Chichester, Walker himself and Baker. In fact, Lundy called none of the Londonderry inhabitants to the meeting apart from John Mogridge, the clerk. Walker and Chichester tried to break in, but were ordered out by Lundy.

Cunningham first handed over King William's letter of instructions. As well as the points mentioned above, Lundy was instructed to make the best defence he could against any persons who attempted to besiege the town or annoy His

Majesty's Protestant citizens and subjects in the neighbouring parts. He was to hinder the enemy from possessing themselves of any passes leading to the city — this he had already signally failed to do — and he was to give all possible aid to any who desired it. He was to receive into the town such Protestant officers and men fit to bear arms as he could rely upon, and form them into disciplined companies. He was, however, to take care not to admit any more useless people — old people, women and children — than there was sufficient provision for.

Finally, Lundy was to co-operate with the two English colonels, the King not doubting 'that the city will continue under our obedience, upon the arrival of an army, which we are sending from England, all things shall be in such a posture, as that we may, with the blessing of God, restore in a short time our Kingdom of Ireland to its former peace and tranquility'.

Lundy, acting as President of the council of war, spoke first. He painted a very gloomy picture of conditions within the city, alleging that provisions could not last longer than a week or ten days at the most, with an enemy 25,000-strong within four or five miles of the walls. He then proposed abandoning the town, intimating that he proposed to quit the place himself, and suggesting that the two regiments should be sent straight back to England. All those present agreed with Lundy's assessment of the situation, with the exception of Colonel Richards, who argued that to abandon Londonderry would mean, in effect, abandoning the Kingdom.

After some discussion, a resolution was passed. One version (Walker's) reads as follows:

> Upon enquiry it seems that there is not provision in the garrison of Londonderry for the present garrison and the two regiments on board, for above a week or ten days at the most: and it appearing that the place is not tenable against a well-appointed army, therefore it is concluded upon and resolved, that it is not convenient for his Majesty's service, but the contrary, to land the two regiments under Colonel Cunningham and Colonel Richards, their command now on

> board on the River of Lough Foyle: that considering the
> present circumstances of affairs and the likelihood the enemy
> will soon possess themselves of this place, it is thought most
> convenient that the principal officers shall privately withdraw
> themselves for their own preservation, as in hopes that the
> inhabitants by a timely capitulation may make terms better
> with the enemy; and that this we judge most convenient for
> His Majesty's service, as the present state of affairs now is.

No independent evidence was sought, and the council
took Lundy's word for it that the town was untenable,
though events were to prove him wrong. The figure of 25,000
troops which he quoted was probably a gross exaggeration,
but even if the number were accurate, the Irish troops were
so ill-equipped and ill-trained as to present no serious
menace. At the subsequent parliamentary inquiry it was
found that there were at that time plenty of provisions in the
town.

It seems that at one stage Lundy had contemplated
destroying all the ammunition left in the city so that it would
not fall into the hands of the enemy. There was talk about an
oath of secrecy. Colonel Richards opposed this and it was
dropped, but the council did agree not to reveal to the
townspeople the decision they had taken. After the meeting,
Cunningham and Richards returned to the ships and
eventually sailed for England.

Lundy's attitude has usually been reckoned to be
treachery but, to be fair, to the military eye Londonderry at
this period may have seemed indefensible. To quote
Macaulay again:

> The fortifications consisted of a simple wall, overgrown with
> grass and weeds: there was no ditch even before the gates: the
> drawbridge had long been neglected: the chains were rusty and
> could scarcely be used: the parapets and towers were built
> after a fashion that might well move disciples of Vauban to
> laughter; and these feeble defences were on almost every side
> commanded by heights. Indeed, those who laid out the city
> never had meant that it should be able to stand a regular siege,
> and had contented themselves with throwing up works
> sufficient to protect the inhabitants against a tumultuary
> attack of the Celtic peasantry. Avaux assured Louvois that a

single French batallion could easily storm such a fastness. Even if the place should, notwithstanding all disadvantages, be able to repel a large army directed by the science and experience of generals who had served under Condé and Turenne, hunger must soon bring the contest to an end. The stock of provisions was small; and the population had been swollen to seven or eight times the ordinary number by a multitude of colonists flying from the rage of the natives.

In Milligan's *History of the Siege of Londonderry*, he prints facts never previously published, taken from the information of Captain Charles Kinaston as to what he knew about Colonel Robert Lundy in the affair of Londonderry. If this material is genuine and true – and it seems strange that Kinaston did not come forward with it at the time of the parliamentary committee of inquiry – it is indeed very damning. Kinaston, according to Milligan, claims that when he was being sent to James to apologize for the fact that he had been fired on from Derry's walls, Lundy called him to a private conference, asking him to explain to James what a faithful servant he (Lundy) had been. He asked Kinaston to mention how he had managed affairs at Cladyford to James's advantage, and told Kinaston about a forged letter – ostensibly from Cunningham – which he had produced for the war council on 17 April. The substance of this letter, Milligan says, was that Cunningham, having considered the state of the garrison, desired and advised Lundy to make the best terms for the town himself, because it was not in a condition to hold out until supplies arrived from England.

Whether this is true or not, during the capitulation negotiations Lundy freely gave out passes to any who wished to leave the town, and the rank and file got so angry at the number of leading officers leaving Londonderry that they shot one of them – a Captain Bell – and wounded another. While James was hurrying to Londonderry, to receive the town's surrender as he thought, a party of townspeople sent Captain Cole to the British ships to offer the Governorship of the town to Colonel Cunningham, if he would only return with his troops. There were plenty of supplies in the town, they told him, and if he would land with his regiments, they

The Reverend Mr GEORGE WALKER
Governeur of LONDON DERRY
The Starenburgh of IRELAND

Above left Colonel John
Michelburne (his name
appears here without the
final 'e', one of the many
different spellings), who was,
on the death of Colonel
Baker, appointed joint
Governor of Londonderry
with the Rev. George
Walker. *Above right* The Rev.
George Walker, who was
joint Governor of
Londonderry throughout the
entire siege and who kept a
diary of events. *Right* Count
Frederick Schomberg, a
German general who had
served in the French army
and who was in overall
charge of King William's
forces in Ireland, though he
himself did not arrive until
after the siege was over.

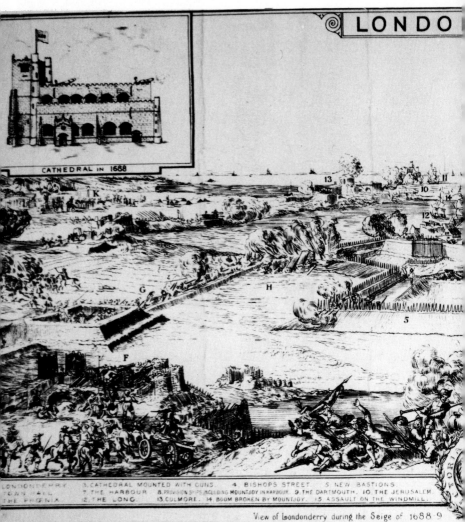

CATHEDRAL IN 1688

LONDONDERRY.   3. CATHEDRAL MOUNTED WITH GUNS.   4. BISHOPS STREET.   5. NEW BASTIONS.
TOWN HALL.   7. THE HARBOUR.   8. PROVISION SHIPS INCLUDING MOUNTJOY IN HARBOUR.   9. THE DARTMOUTH.   10. THE JERUSALEM.
THE PHOENIX.   12. THE LONG.   13. CULMORE.   14. BOOM BROKEN BY MOUNTJOY.   15. ASSAULT ON THE WINDMILL.

View of Londonderry during the Seige of 1688·9

LONDONDERRY, MAP OF THE SIEGE, 1689

A-B KIRKES FLEET   C. IRISHMEN SURPRISED BY THE INHABITANTS OF INCH.   D ARRIVAL OF THE IRISHMEN.
E.   SORTIE AGAINST THE IRISHMEN & THEIR DEFEAT. F FRENCH WORKS INCOMPLETE. G. FRENCH APPROACHES. H. FRENCH WORKS DESTROYED.
I.   FRENCH & IRISH FIGHTING.   K CRUELTIES OF KING JAMES & D'AVAUX EXECUTED ON THE CLERGY.

from an Engraving by Romeyn de Hooghe

A general view of Londonderry during the siege, from an engraving by
Romeyn de Hooghe. This view is from the Bogside looking roughly from
the west. Many of the details are quite inaccurate; it was usual in this period
for engravers to adapt existing drawings of sieges by inserting a few
recognisable details, but the windmill can clearly be seen just outside the city
walls on the right, as can the fortified position outside the walls which was
occupied by the defenders of Londonderry. The cathedral, with its square
tower and Michelburne's bloody flag, is clearly visible. Kirke's fleet appears
on the horizon. The confused foreground purports to illustrate some of the
incidents from the siege.

Above Attack—Jacobite forces firing on the city with cannon and mortar from behind fascines (basket-work 'blockhouses' filled with earth). This view, from a contemporary engraving, is depicted from the west; Kirke's fleet can be seen on the horizon. *Below* Defence—the citizens of Londonderry manning the walls. The square tower of the cathedral with Michelburne's flag flying from it is visible in the background. This is an idealized Victorian reconstruction.

would march out and tackle the enemy, leaving his men to garrison the city. Cunningham refused the offer and sent back a message that the people would be well advised to obey Governor Lundy.

When the ships moved down the Lough, the townspeople knew that the rumours they had been hearing of Lundy's determination to surrender the town were true; on 18 April, Mogridge, the clerk, let it be known that the council had decided on 16 April to send the ships back to England and to keep news of this from the populace. Following the surrender negotiations of 17 April, the townspeople kept a close watch on Lundy's house so that he was now for all practical purposes a prisoner and could not escape to the ships which were waiting for him. Realizing this, Lundy smuggled a message out to Cunningham, begging him not to leave without him 'lest he become a sacrifice to the rabble'. On 18 April, the ships moved down to Greencastle, and on 19 April sailed for England without Lundy.

With the ships gone, Lundy's position became even more perilous. While the parleys were going on, a new leader had appeared on the scene. Adam Murray, one of the prominent Protestants in the district and a soldier, advanced with a large party of horse from Culmore Fort to Pennyburn Mill, within sight of the walls. Lundy was alarmed that the appearance of Murray's horse on the scene might upset the surrender negotiations, and sent a relative of Murray's out to order his men back out of sight of the city. The messenger explained to Murray what had been happening in Londonderry and Murray decided, instead of going back to Culmore, to enter the town with his forces and help to defend it. Lundy refused him admittance, but James Morrison, Captain of the Guards, opened up the city to Murray and his troops.

While the Governor and the war council were still trying to arrange surrender terms, Murray went through the streets urging the citizens to resist, pointing out to them that Londonderry was now the last Protestant stronghold in Ireland and warning them that unless the traitor Lundy and his cabal were expelled, everything they had already suffered would be in vain. Murray, encouraged by other officers, then said that all who were prepared to fight on should tie a white handkerchief around their left arms. This was followed by a proclamation at the guard that all loyal and true citizens should parade with a white handkerchief tied around their left arms. Within a short time there were several thousand people on parade all wearing white handkerchiefs and proclaiming their determination to hold the city, regardless of Lundy's negotiations.

Led by Murray, a party of the townsfolk then broke in on the council meeting. In the meantime, the council had decided to try to persuade Murray to sign the instrument of surrender, so that when he burst in he was asked to explain his attitude to Lundy. He replied that Lundy was either a fool or a knave and gave his reasons for this statement, instancing some recent events — Lundy's abandonment of Tyrone to the enemy, his negligent planning of the defence of the passes and his desertion of the passes with an army of 10,000 men willing and able to fight. Unbelievably, Lundy continued to try to persuade Murray to sign the instrument of surrender.

Storming out of the meeting, Murray communicated what had happened to the citizens, who were eagerly awaiting new developments. He told them that the Governor and the council were determined to give up the city, and added that if they did this, it would be impossible to hold on at Culmore. After consultation, he decided to stay on in the town and do everything in his power to prevent Lundy and the council from handing it over.

Meanwhile the council were considering the best means of getting an instrument of surrender out of the city to King James. In view of the temper of the townsfolk this clearly wasn't going to be easy. At one stage during the deliberations of the council, Lundy sent for all the non-Conformist ministers in the city, hoping that their presence at the council might make the mob change its mind since, as we have seen, most of it was non-Conformist by persuasion. It is doubtful whether this ruse would have worked, but in the event the non-Conformist ministers declined Lundy's invitation to attend, and his war council never met again. Lundy took to his chamber and stayed there, guarded by redcoats.

The townspeople of Londonderry now started to look

around for a successor to Lundy as Governor. They turned first to Adam Murray who had emerged as a natural leader during the surrender negotiations. Murray refused the honour because he felt that his talents would be more useful to the garrison in the field. The choice for Governor then fell on two men, Major Henry Baker, a soldier, and the Rev. George Walker, Rector of Donoughmore, Co. Tyrone, a clergyman and amateur soldier; he was the man who had ridden into Londonderry (see page 76) to arrange to keep communications open between the city and the two regiments he had raised at Dungannon. Baker was aged about forty-two and Walker forty-three, and there appears to be some doubt as to their position *vis-à-vis* one another. According to Mackenzie, a council was called for the purpose of electing a Governor to succeed Lundy. The persons nominated were Major Henry Baker, Major Michelburne and Lieutenant-Colonel Richard Johnston. Major Baker received a majority of the votes and was elected. He then asked if he could have an assistant to handle the administration of the stores and was allowed to nominate his own assistant; he chose Walker. Mackenzie admits that Walker was also referred to as Governor, but it was always understood, he says, that this was merely in respect of the stores. Michelburne — in *Ireland Preserv'd, or the Siege of Londonderry,* his tragi-comedy in two parts and five acts published in London in 1705 — described Lundy as Londonderry's first Governor, Baker as the city's second Governor, and himself as third Governor, and he refers to Walker as 'Walker that went under the name of one of the Governors'.

According to Walker's own account, he and Baker were chosen as joint Governors. Captain Joseph Bennet, writing his *True and Impartial Account* shortly after the siege, concurs; he says that the city unanimously chose Baker and Walker to be joint Governors, with Murray to be General in the Field, in charge of sallies outside the walls. Ash, in his journal of the siege, says that the Governorship of the city was conferred on two worthy gentlemen, Walker and Baker. Captain George Holmes, Captain Charles Kinaston and Gervais Squire are all agreed that there were two Governors; Gervais Squire, who was Mayor of Londonderry, certified that he administered the oath to both of them as Governors, Walker having precedence. King William III, King James II and the Jacobite leaders seem to have regarded Walker as sole Governor. The matter is not of any great importance except to illustrate how much confusion exists over details about which there could hardly be any dispute; it is unusual, to say the least, to find people who lived in a city throughout a siege at loggerheads as to who was in fact Governor of the place at the time.

After the Governor, or Governors, had been chosen, the garrison was formed into eight regiments, and colonels were appointed. The soldiers, by now largely deserted by their officers, chose captains from the ranks, and each captain decided under which colonel he would serve, a curiously democratic way of ordering matters. The Governors ordered that two regiments should remain on guard every night, and proceeded to make other arrangements for the defence of the city. They stipulated that there should be no drinking after eight o'clock at night or candles lighted which might direct enemy fire. Another regulation stated that the soldiers were each to have a salmon and a half, two pounds of salt beef and four quarts of oatmeal a week, pretty generous rations for a beleaguered city and an indication that Lundy was not being truthful when he said that there were not supplies in the place for more than a week or ten days. Another regulation stipulated that inn-keepers were not to take more than a penny a quart for beer, since the soldiers were not receiving any pay.

The ammunition was taken from the main store and housed in four different locations in case of fire or treachery. All stores belonging to merchants who had left the town were commandeered and placed in the communal stores, and inventories were taken to guard against plundering. The drummers were instructed to lodge in one house so that they would be readily accessible to sound the alarm, at which the soldiers would take their places on the ramparts.

While all these preparations were going ahead, Lundy was allowed to escape from the city. Walker and Baker, out of the respect they held for the commission he carried, contributed to his escape by allowing him to disguise himself as a private soldier, carrying a load of match – prepared cord for firing a gun – on his back, in a sally for the relief of Culmore. The match was used for firing muskets and some of the soldiers carried reserve supplies; Lundy posed as one of these match-carriers. Perhaps it was the fact that he carried this match on his back which gave rise to earlier accounts of the escape, mentioned among others by Macaulay, that he escaped disguised as a porter. There also used to be a legend that he escaped by climbing down from a pear tree in the orchard outside the East Wall, which was one of the sights of the city until it was uprooted by a storm in 1844.

On reaching Culmore, Lundy escaped to Scotland where he was arrested and put in the Tower of London, on suspicion of 'treasonable practices against His Majesty's Government'. The warrant, signed by Lord Shrewsbury, is dated 13 May 1689.

On 3 June it was resolved, according to the Journal of the House of Commons,* that His Majesty be desired to give direction that copies of the Commissions and Instructions given in relation to Londonderry and the Kingdom of Ireland be transmitted to a committee appointed to inquire into the miscarriages at Londonderry, and also that Colonel Lundy, a prisoner in the Tower, be brought before this committee.

It was 12 August before Sir Thomas Littleton was able to report the conclusions of this committee, which had examined a number of witnesses.

He reported that Lord Kingston had given evidence about the dispersal of his forces at Lundy's instructions which resulted in the breaking up of the best body of horse which the Protestants had. Lundy had promised to send forces and guns to make Dungannon a frontier town against Charlemont, five miles away. Upon this information, he said, the country people had fortified Dungannon and brought in a great store of provisions; yet on 16 March Lundy had given orders to quit the town with the result that the provisions were left behind and taken by the enemy, who were in bad

---

*A summary appears in the anonymous history of Derry in John Hempton's anthology *The Siege and History of Londonderry* published in 1861.

need of supplies.

The committee had heard that Lundy took the oath to be true to King William on board James Hamilton's ship, whereupon his commission was delivered to him. Sir Arthur Royden had informed the committee that he and Captain Beverly, who commanded the *Jersey* frigate, and several others were put out of the cabin at that time on the grounds that Lundy and Mr Hamilton had private business to discuss, but that Mr Hamilton said later that Lundy had been sworn. The next day, when most of the officers and gentry took the oath, Lundy was asked to take it again but refused.

Mr James Hamilton had attested that Colonel Lundy assisted at the swearing in of other members of the garrison and in the proclamation of King William on 22 March.

Further evidence had been given that Hamilton had delivered all the arms and ammunition he had brought with him plus £595 16s 8d, which was all he had been able to raise of the £1,000 he was supposed to provide for Lundy.

The committee had heard that on 15 April, all Protestants from sixteen to sixty were ordered to meet to defend the passes at Cladyford, Lifford and Long Causey to stop the enemy from advancing further towards Londonderry, and that Lundy had marched out with a great part of the garrison on that date.

Lord Blaney had given evidence that when the enemy approached the passes, the Protestants ran in great confusion. No orders were given or observed. Lundy was looked upon as Commander-in-Chief but few of the men had any powder and they were routed before three rounds were fired.

David Cairnes had given evidence to the effect that he believed the enemy knew their intentions for they went immediately to the place where the Protestants had arranged to meet. He had acquainted Lundy of this and urged him to march immediately but Lundy had refused to move until 10 a.m. on the Monday morning.

Major Joseph Stroud had advised that harrows be thrown into the river at Cladyford to hinder the enemy but this was not done, and Captain Bennet had given evidence that there was no breastwork or other defence at any of the passes.

The parliamentary report went on to recount events

following the arrival in the river of Colonel Cunningham and Colonel Richards with the first relief force (they arrived on the day of the fight at Cladyford). It had considered the letters which had passed between Cunningham and Lundy and heard of the meeting from which Lundy excluded 'divers of the officers who did use to come to former Councils, particularly Colonel Hamilton, Colonel Chichester, Major Walker and Major Baker'. The committee found that Lundy had made a proposition to quit the town and send the two regiments back again, on the grounds that there were not enough provisions in the place for more than a week or ten days; and that all present had subscribed to a paper consenting to quit the town, agreeing on their honour not to disclose the decision.

Cornet Nicholson had attested that at the time this decision was taken there was a great store of provisions in the town and ships were arriving daily with stores. Shortly afterwards the ships sailed without Lundy, who escaped to Scotland later disguised as a private soldier.

Colonel Lundy had been several times examined by the committee and admitted that he fled from the passes but claimed that it was because the men would not fight. He had also admitted that he had locked the gates of Londonderry but said it was because he was afraid the rabble would get in and make inroads into their already scarce supplies of food. He had admitted to all the proceedings at the council of war but claimed that he genuinely believed that provisions were as scarce as he said they were. Cunningham and Richards had also been examined; Richards, it was found, had merely obeyed orders.

Lundy had many influential friends who tried not only to prevent him from being sent to Londonderry for trial, but to have him released. He was still in prison in October 1689 and on 22 October he petitioned the House of Commons that he might be tried in England and not in Londonderry. He also argued his innocence, and, in all fairness, he had a case: if he had really been a traitor working for King James for a reward, he would hardly have fled from Culmore to Scotland, but would have escaped instead to King James to claim the reward.

Before the House of Commons had reached a decision on this matter, his case came up under *habeas corpus* and he was 'admitted to bail'.

Nothing then seems to be known about his movements until August 1704 when he applied to the Lord High Treasurer for an advance in pay to enable him to go to Portugal to serve as adjutant-general there; he was given £108. It would appear that his influential friends had succeeded in getting the hearing of his case delayed indefinitely. Later he was sent to assist Prince George of Hesse Darmstadt and figured in the defence of Gibraltar against the French and Spaniards who were besieging it. (Incidentally, Leake, who had commanded the Fleet at the time of the relief of Londonderry, played a prominent part in assisting the defence of Gibraltar.)

Lundy was taken prisoner in April 1707 and in June 1709 he and several other officers were exchanged for French prisoners of war (Lundy was exchanged for twenty-five men). He returned that month to England where he seems to have lived in obscurity until his death, around 1717.

Ever since the siege, he has been execrated by the people of Londonderry, who developed a tradition of burning him in effigy, wearing his cocked hat and gold epaulettes and bearing the legend LUNDY THE TRAITOR, on the anniversary of the closing of the gates. The practice began in 1789 on the centenary of the siege and before long it was taken over by the Derry Apprentice Boys, an association of men who meet to perpetuate the memory of the original 'brave thirteen' who closed the gates. The effigy, normally about sixteen feet high and weighing about a ton, used to be burned at the Governor Walker memorial until that was destroyed, during the current troubles.

VIII   *Londonderry under siege*

When the Protestants decided to defend Londonderry, they were influenced by the knowledge that the fort of Culmore was also in Protestant hands and would not only offer the city a measure of protection but could also ensure that the river was kept free for the relief of the city by water. In enemy hands Culmore fort might be a serious menace to the city and could be used to prevent supplies of men and material reaching the city by sea.

Accordingly, when the Irish army came before Londonderry, one of its first objectives was to capture the fort. Before the siege started, Warham Jemmet had been appointed captain of Culmore by Lundy, but when the Irish forces approached Culmore he was ordered to evacuate it: yet another circumstance which is quoted as a further proof of Lundy's treachery. The Irish then took possession of it, but it was recaptured by the Protestant horse returning from Cladyford and unable, as we have seen, to gain admission to Londonderry. Murray was among the officers who recaptured the fort. Murray then went into Londonderry, and the garrison at Culmore sent a deputation to King James at Strabane, where he had retired from St Johnston on the morning of 20 April. James agreed to pardon the garrison and give them his protection if they would agree to surrender the fort. The following day the fort was surrendered to King James, though his forces never made full use of it; if they had, Londonderry might not have been relieved.

On the surrender of the fort, Maumont, Hamilton, Pusignan and Berwick advanced 400 foot, Tyrconnel's regiment of cavalry and some dragoons, making about 700 horse in all, and took their quarters around Culmore. The Culmore garrison were permitted to retire to Londonderry, taking their arms and ammunition with them. The officers and men were all granted a free pardon and were allowed to depart with all their belongings, including their swords and pistols; the officers were even permitted to keep their horses. This lenience was perhaps intended to serve as an example to the citizens of Londonderry and to show them the sort of treatment they might expect if they, too, agreed to surrender. In fact, the articles of surrender for the fort of Culmore included a statement to the effect that 'if the Gentlemen, Officers and Soldiers of Londonderry accept the like favour of His Majesty, they may enjoy the same if they accept it within three days and surrender the garrison'.

It was rumoured afterwards that as Lundy passed through Culmore on his way to Scotland, he dropped a hint that Londonderry had already surrendered, to weaken the resolve of the garrison at Culmore, but it is difficult to see what advantage he would have in doing this if he were going to Scotland and not to King James to seek reward from that quarter. It is possible, of course, that Lundy genuinely believed that Londonderry could not hold out for long, and that the Protestants in the city would get a better deal if they surrendered. Viewed in this light, many of his seemingly inexplicable actions begin to make some sort of sense.

King James's forces now put about 100 men into the fort at Culmore and seized all the boats on the River Foyle.

A few days earlier, on 21 April, at Omagh, James had entertained a deputation from the Protestant garrison of Derg Castle – now Castlederg – which stands on a narrow pass between Enniskillen and Londonderry. They offered to surrender on condition that they should be spared their goods and their lives. This request was granted and yet another Protestant stronghold which could have inconvenienced the Irish army greatly in its efforts to besiege Londonderry was eliminated without any resistance.

Meanwhile the inhabitants of Londonderry continued with their plans to defend the town. Most of the houses outside the walls were burned down and the rubble levelled so that the besiegers could not take cover there, and Alderman Tomlin's orchard and the hedge around it were razed for the same reason. Two guns brought from Culmore were mounted on the cathedral tower, which was without a spire, and these guns commanded the whole area around the town.

Fearing that King William, on learning that Cunningham and Richards had not in fact landed their men, might assume that the city was now lost and would not send any further assistance, the citizens appointed Captain Joseph Bennet — author of *A True and Impartial Account*, published in 1689 — to make his way through the Irish camp and try to get word to King William that the city was as determined as ever to hold out. To deceive the Irish army into thinking that he was a traitor escaping, some of the garrison posted near the windmill fired some shots over his head as he left the town. The enemy took him for a deserter and held him prisoner for a time; later he made his way to Scotland and thence to England to make his report to King William.

According to Walker, the number of men, women and children in the city at the beginning of the siege proper was about 30,000 but when the Irish army declared that it would receive and protect any who deserted, about 10,000, he says, left the city. Of the remaining 20,000, about 7,000 were fighting men, formed into eight regiments of 117 companies, each consisting of 60 men. This doesn't in fact add up mathematically — but most of the statistics furnished by the various chroniclers of Londonderry are equally unreliable. In addition, Walker says that there were 341 officers and three unregimented or independent companies — which may account for the discrepancy. But the numbers both of fighting men and of citizens in Londonderry fluctuated wildly throughout the siege as some people deserted the city, while others flocked into it.

Reports as to the number of men in the field besieging Londonderry vary as much if not more. Writing of the Irish dispositions at the beginning of the siege proper, Bennet — who, as we have seen, was held in the Irish camp for a time, before he left for Scotland — says that the Irish were quartered from St Johnston for about eight miles in distance. These forces, he said, did not amount to more than 7,000 on the Derry side. On the other side of the water, he gives the probable total as 3,000 near Strong's Orchard (see map on page 7), with several cannon in view of the town.

Belloc puts the numbers under the walls variously between 6,000 and 10,000. Hamilton says that there were six battalions, the best of which had 600 and the worst 400. The Duke of Berwick has it that at the beginning of the siege there were over nine battalions of foot and four regiments of horse at Londonderry for the siege.

So, on the whole, it seems probable that there were between 10,000 and 17,000 Irish troops before Londonderry at the start of the operations. Only one contemporary Jacobite narrative of the war puts the number of Irish forces as high as 20,000, but even if this figure is correct, there doesn't seem to be much doubt that the Irish army was so ill-equipped and -officered that not more than 10,000 of these could be regarded as effective at any given moment.

James still had not given up all hopes of inducing the citizens to surrender peaceably. On 20 April, he sent the Earl of Abercorn, one of the few Catholic peers in Ireland, to treat with the besieged. Strabane was met outside the gates by Adam Murray. He told Murray that he had been authorized to promise the citizens a free pardon for all that had happened if they would submit themselves to their lawful sovereign, King James. Murray himself was offered a Colonel's commission in the Irish Army, plus £1,000 in cash (worth about £8,800 today), if he would agree to these terms, but Murray answered: 'The men of Londonderry have done nothing that requires a pardon, and own no sovereign but King William and Queen Mary.'

James now returned disconsolately to Dublin, and the garrison of Londonderry settled in for the siege. All parties were urged to forget their religious differences for the time being. The eighteen Church of Ireland and the eight non-Conformist ministers worked round the clock to keep up the spirits of the besieged and as a rare, early example of ecumenism, it was decided that the Church of Ireland congregations should have the use of the cathedral on Sunday mornings, and that the non-Conformists should be allowed to take it over during Sunday afternoon.

Maumont had established his headquarters near Culmore. On the night of 21—22 April, he sent orders to Brigadier Ramsey to occupy the village of Pennyburn (see map on page 7), with a detachment of foot under Colonel Hamilton. On Sunday morning, 21 April, Colonel Murray in Londonderry saw the men on the march, and sent out 500 musketeers in small parties to line the hedges along the road leading from the city to Pennyburn. Murray formed his horse into two troops of 100 each, leading one troop himself and putting the other under the command of Major Nathaniel Bull. By the time Hamilton had taken possession of Pennyburn, Murray had ordered a second party of musketeers to seize some high ground overlooking the area. Hamilton, alarmed by the appearance of this force, sent an urgent appeal to Maumont for reinforcements. Maumont immediately hurried to Hamilton's assistance with all the cavalry he could raise – a troop of forty men. Picking up a troop of dragoons on the way, Maumont led this party at full gallop from Culmore to Pennyburn. At Pennyburn, he encountered Murray's forces and was killed. The Londonderry horse were then forced back within the walls of the city by Berwick.

The Irish cavalry suffered heavy losses as they galloped past the hedges lined by Protestant musketeers. Both Walker and Mackenzie agree that the enemy losses in this skirmish were around 200. Bennet puts the figure at about 60 killed, including Maumont and some other officers. The casualties among the Londonderry men were much lighter, probably no more than three officers and half a dozen men killed. Apart from the fact that Maumont, one of the principal officers of the besieging army, was killed in this engagement, the Irish lost a large quantity of arms and equipment. From that day onwards, the Londonderry garrison was always ready to sally out and do battle with the besiegers, usually inflicting heavy casualties on them and invariably returning laden down with booty taken from their foes.

The Londonderry dead were buried with full military honours. Although some doubt has been cast on it, it seems possible that Maumont was killed by Murray in a personal, hand-to-hand, conflict. An eighteenth-century tapestry depicts Murray in the act of slaying Maumont.

On 21 April, the Irish army placed a demi-culverin – a long cannon firing a ball about 9 lbs in weight – on the other side of the river and about 1,000 yards from the town. With this they soon began firing but did little damage except to a few houses in the town.

On 22 April, they placed four demi-culverins at the lower end of Strong's Orchard, on the opposite side of the river and facing Shipquay Street. With these they fired cannon balls at houses inside the city walls. The besieged replied with fire from two bastions, killing a Colonel O'Neal, two sergeants, some soldiers and two friars. What the friars were doing on the battlefield the contemporary accounts do not say; presumably they were ministering to the Irish forces.

The besiegers reinforced their post at Pennyburn and on 25 April Colonel Murray tried to drive them off. The action began at nine o'clock in the morning and lasted all day. It would have gone badly for the besiegers if Brigadier Ramsey had not arrived at about 7 p.m. with reinforcements. When Ramsey's four battalions arrived, the besieged, who had been on the attack, retired behind Londonderry's walls. During the attack, the French Major-General Pusignan was badly wounded and Berwick himself received his only wound of the campaign. Pusignan died later through lack of proper medical attention, a fact which was glumly reported to King Louis by Avaux.

This was the last occasion on which Murray's horse proved consequential in the defence of the city. By now forage was becoming extremely scare and the horses began to be killed off to supplement the rations of the garrison.

The besiegers reinforced their artillery in Strong's Orchard with some mortar pieces and on the night of 27–28 April fired some small bombs, which did little damage, into the city. The Governors ordered that part of the pavements of the city should be pulled up lest bombs, striking them, should cause them to fly about injuring people. They also decided to barricade the upper part of Shipquay Street with timber, stones, and manure, to protect it from cannon fire.

Three bombs struck the Market House, damaging the clock and removing some slates. The Irish army now stepped up their bombardment of the city and it was soon on fire in several places. Roofs and upper stories of many houses fell in and several people were crushed to death. At first many of the inhabitants, none of whom had seen the effect of such a cannonade on a crowded city, were demoralized by the crashing of chimney stacks and the heaps of ruins punctuated here and there with disfigured corpses. But, as always, familiarity with danger and horror soon produced a sort of callous indifference and life within the besieged city went on.

Throughout the siege, there were constant fears of what in later terminology was called a 'fifth column' at work within the city. Even as early as this, hearing rumours that spies and enemies within the town might be attempting to undermine the walls in order to make it easier for the Irish army to penetrate the defences, Governor Baker and Mr William Mackie, under pretence of checking on stores, searched all the cellars in the town but found nothing amiss.

With Maumont dead, Hamilton was now in complete charge of the siege. His next move was to resort to the most extraordinary stratagem in the hope of getting Colonel Murray to surrender. Learning that Murray's eighty-year-old father lived a short distance from the city at Cumber, Co. Londonderry, Hamilton sent a party to bring the old man to his camp at Brookhall. Murray's father was quite unperturbed when Hamilton told him that his son was in rebellion against the King and was forcing the people of Londonderry to hold out against their will. Hamilton asked Murray's father to advise his son to desist and reinforced his request with the threat that if he didn't do so, he would be hanged forthwith. Murray the elder warned Hamilton that he was sure his son would never disown his allegiance to King William but agreed to be taken to Londonderry to see his son. Father and son greeted each other with affection and Murray the elder exhorted his son not to give in, then returned to Hamilton and reported that nothing would force his son to quit the town or surrender to King James.

Windmill Hill, situated about 500 yards south of Bishop's Gate, was held by the besieged. There were some guns mounted in this enclosed area, and these were supplemented by riflemen using long fowling pieces which greatly troubled the besiegers. These fowling pieces were flintlocks with a longer range than the ordinary matchlock musket.

Hamilton, who had been advised that some heavy battering guns had been despatched from Dublin for him, now made up his mind to seize this hill and so secure a good position for this new artillery. On the night of 5–6 May, Ramsey's brigade made a surprise attack on the hill with a battalion of Guards, Ramsey's own regiment and various other units, in all about 3,000 men. Governor Baker realized the seriousness of this attack and sent out a strong force to attack the Irish infantry, who were holding a line of trenches which Ramsey had made in the ditches around the hill. After a short and furious fight, Ramsey's men gave way and fled, leaving some of their arms behind them. Ramsey made a stout attempt to rally his men but was shot down in the process, and the rout continued. Nearly a dozen Jacobite officers were lost in this action. Both Walker and Mackenzie reckon that the Irish lost about 200 men killed and that about 500 were wounded, of whom a further 300 died within the course of the next few days. The Irish army were living in grave discomfort in tents and trenches and the medical services available to them were grossly inadequate.

The wounded prisoners were brought into the town and treated with great respect, being accommodated in private houses and not in the jail. Ramsey was buried in the Long Tower with full military honours, 'much lamented by all who knew him,' Ash says, 'for he was reckoned to be the best soldier in the Irish army next to Colonel Richard Hamilton'.

On the evening of the battle the Governors of the city sent a drum to the Irish camp requesting Hamilton to send an officer and fourteen men to the battlefield to bury their dead. The garrison losses in this encounter were extremely light, probably not more than four or five killed and a few wounded. Five pairs of colours were taken by the besieged during the battle, and two of them, which had been captured by Colonel Michelburne during the fighting, were hung up in the cathedral.

King James was very upset at the death of Ramsey and now promised Hamilton that he would send him a great mortar and two pieces of artillery by land, and the same number by sea, and added that ten companies would soon join him, all well armed and equipped. 'I think it absolutely necessary,' he wrote, 'you should not let any more men come out of Derry, but for intelligence, or some extraordinary occasion, for they may want provisions and be glad to rid themselves of useless mouths.'

On the evening of 7 May, there was a slight skirmish near Pennyburn, but little was achieved on either side though three or four of the garrison were killed and eight wounded, two of whom died the following day.

Early on 11 May, over 1,000 soldiers of the garrison went from Windmill Hill towards Pennyburn, in the hope of surprising the enemy in their tents and driving them out of the area. Two cannon in the neighbourhood were fired on them, but there were no casualties. After a time, the besieged, realizing that there was no prospect of achieving their aims, returned to the city. On the same night, the Irish army fired into the town, and the garrison returned the fire from the walls, killing the Jacobite officer in charge. This was the sort of minor engagement that marked the progress of time in May and June.

Reference has already been made to the fortified area around the mill which remained in the hands of the besieged. In addition to this, Governor Baker now decided to draw a line of fortifications from the bog, across Windmill Hill to the river, and to secure it with redoubts to protect his men from the gun battery which the Irish army had placed on the opposite side of the river (see map on page 7). As a result of these fortifications, a considerable area of the land immediately under the walls to the south of the city was in the hands of the besieged, who also controlled the Shipquay, so that the impression given by many accounts of the siege of 30,000 Protestants pinned within the walls for 105 days is entirely false. Walker says that the number of guns placed on the bastions and other fortifications was eight sakers – small cannon – and twelve demi-culverins. The market house in the Diamond was turned into a guardhouse and the principal magazine was to the north-west of the town, on the site of the old castle which Sir Henry Dowcra had fortified. Nevill says that it was very exposed and Walker was of the opinion that most of the houses in the town were exposed to the enemy guns.

According to Bennet there was a gun planted by the besieged within twenty yards of each of the four gates, all of which led to the market square, one directly against each gate, to clear the streets. There was a dry ditch around the town over which there were two drawbridges, one at Bishop's Gate and the other at Ferryquay Gate, but in some places these ditches were filled in. There were some wells within the town, but the main wells were outside the city walls.

Orders were given after the battle of Windmill Hill on 6 May that every regiment was to mount guard by turns, night and day, at the new line, but later, owing to suspicions aroused by the behaviour of an officer, it was decided that the guard would consist of two detachments from each regiment. Michelburne in his tragi-comedy *Ireland Preserved* states that Hamilton was in daily correspondence with 'fifth-columinists' inside the town and asserts that up to thirty people a day were deserting. Avaux reported to Louis XIV that Hamilton was allowing between fifty and a hundred people a day to leave Londonderry, against King James's express orders.

With the arrival of the artillery which King James had promised Hamilton, there was a distinct change in the character of the bombardment of the town, which now grew far more intense, though it was never intense by modern standards. Over the whole period of the siege, Walker gives a total of 587 bombs thrown into the city, as against Ash's estimate of 584, a remarkably slight discrepancy.

On 3 June the bombardment was stepped up, 28 large bombs being discharged into the city on that day. Between 3 June and 8 June inclusive, 159 bombs were hurled into the crowded city. Ash gives some details of the effects of this bombing. The 36 bombs which fell on the night of 4 June killed many people. One fell on David Cairnes's house, went through to the cellar where some of Ash's men lay ill, and killed two of them and wounded others. A bomb fell on a Mr Moore's house which drove out a stone and this in turn killed a man at the Shipquay bastion. A bomb from a mortar killed

Dr Alexander Lindsay, surgeon to Colonel Walker's regiment, who had done much good work attending the sick and wounded. Another which fell on the old churchyard of St Augustine raised five corpses out of their graves and threw them over the church wall. They were immediately re-interred. Many of the sick, being unable to leave their houses, were killed, and one result of the bombardment, according to Walker, was that people could not enjoy their rest and thus became faint and more easily subject to disease. On the other hand, one advantage of the destruction of so many houses was that timber, which had been very scarce, became available for fuel.

Towards the end of May, Mackenzie reported, some of the officers in the town grew suspicious of Walker. There were allegations that he had been attempting to surrender the town, to sell or embezzle the stores, and even to betray the city for money. But Walker continued as Governor throughout the siege and Edward Curling, Keeper of the Stores, declares that Walker did not embezzle any of the stores. It seems that a good deal of what Mackenzie had to say against Walker was pure prejudice, possibly the prejudice of the Presbyterian of that period against the established Church of Ireland.

For some weeks after the battle of Windmill Hill, little of note occurred in the town beyond its bombing by the Irish army and various skirmishing raids on the part of the garrison. Walker attributes this inactivity to the lack of courage on the part of the Irish army, and to the garrison's lack of horse.

The sallies were usually begun by small parties acting on their own initiative. What would apparently happen was that an officer would see some Irish troops approaching the town and would run out accompanied by a dozen or so men. When the other besieged saw them thus engaged and in danger, they would go out in greater numbers to their assistance, and a sort of pitched battle would result. It all seems to have been very casual and highly disorganized. In addition, there were constant small, spontaneous sallies out to attack the miserable besiegers who were under-armed, deadly ill, without proper medical supplies or attention, living in tents and shallow trenches in abominable weather.

About the middle of May, the besiegers moved their main body from St Johnston and pitched their tents at Balloughry Hill, two miles to the south-southwest of the town. Next they established additional camps at Pennyburn Mill and at the orchard on the other side of the river. They placed guards all round the town, and along both banks of the river, so that the besieged began to find it more difficult to receive or convey intelligence. Until this moment, they had been able to send out messengers who could convey information about the position of the city, or bring in news concerning affairs in the Irish camp. This latest move by the Irish army also made it more difficult for the besieged to reach St Columb's Wells, which were just beyond the walls on the west side of the city, on which the inhabitants drew largely for their water supplies.

The supply of water inside the town itself was so muddy that the garrison and inhabitants frequently had to run the hazard of going out to St Columb's Wells under the enemy guns, an operation which involved many casualties. (Incidentally, the wells are still there today, in the district known as the Bogside.) The besieged erected a small redoubt to hinder the besiegers and protect people going to the wells, and the besiegers dug a trench from which they could fire on the inhabitants as they approached the wells.

After the Irish army had established their new camp at Balloughry, they ranged themselves in a long line in all their camps and opened fire on the besieged, presumably to give the impression of enormous firing strength and in the hope of striking terror into the hearts of the garrison. They made forts and trenches, piling up fascines — barricades of brushwood faggots — in some places, and erected a trench near Pennyburn Mill and planted some guns there.

On 27 May, 300 of the garrison went out at daybreak from the Windmill, half of them going to Balloughry and the other half to Pennyburn, in the hope of surprising the enemy camps. There was no action worth speaking about at Balloughry but the Pennyburn raid was a lively one and some lives were lost in the fray.

Murray led another raiding party towards Brookhall, where

he burnt a number of the enemy out of their trenches and destroyed their fascines. There was a lot of confused skirmishing in and out of the trenches and a few lives were lost, but the period in the main was so uneventful that historians pick on such minor incidents as the cannon which fired up Pump Street on 13 May and took the leg off one boy and wounded another.

On Tuesday 21 May, the non-Conformists in the city held a solemn feast and collections were taken for the poor, who were beginning to feel the pinch. Soon after this, according to Mackenzie, the Conformists held their special day of feasting. As supplies of food in the city were now growing extremely scarce, we can take it that these were feasts largely in the symbolic sense.

On 29 May, according to Ash's Journal, the besieged learnt of the Jacobite plan to bombard the town still more intensely and accordingly they buried 107 barrels of powder in dried-up wells in Bishop Street and warned inhabitants to have water ready at all times to put out fires started by the bombs.

On the following day a messenger was captured and the besieged learned from letters he was carrying that the Irish army had lost 3,000 men from enemy action and from sickness since the siege began, and that they could get no rest because of the frequent sallies of the beseiged. They also learned that a large army was expected from England or Scotland to relieve Londonderry, and this news was celebrated by firing the great guns and by ringing the cathedral bells.

During the night the Irish army began to make trenches in the hills on the far side of the bog; they placed a cannon at Strawbridge's town and another at Tanneymore on the other side of the river, opposite the Windmill.

On the last day of May there was another skirmish at the Windmill but again it proved inconclusive.

Three years before the siege the cathedral steeple with its leaden roof had been taken down because it was in need of repairs which the city could not afford; the lead now came in very handy for making bullets and shot to fire against the besiegers. A red flag, known as Michelburne's bloody flag, had been flown from the square tower of the cathedral throughout the siege as a sign of the town's defiance, and this crimson colour has ever since been worn by the Derry Apprentice Boys.

By the end of May the besiegers had crept up so close to the walls that the garrison could hardly venture outside the city bounds except to the enclosed area around the Windmill. The besiegers then began the more systematic bombing which had been threatened. During the six days of 3–8 June, as mentioned above, a total of 159 bombs were lobbed into the city.

In Dublin King James was still resolved to press forward with the siege and was greatly distressed at the reports which reached him of the continuing resistance of Londonderry and Enniskillen.* About the beginning of June he received news that 'the great guns and mortars arrived not in the camp until the thirtieth of May, and till then, little was done against the town except beating them back when they ventured to sally and firing with what guns we had upon them'.

Part of the new policy of a closer siege was the decision to capture the garrison's entrenchments at Windmill Hill and the surrounding area, the only ground outside the city walls now effectively held by the Protestants. The Irish army assembled their troops, then consisting in all, according to Berwick, of about 5,000 to 6,000 men, and encamped in front of the hill and behind a rise in the ground about the distance of a long musket shot away, leaving on the other side of the river two battalions which had been stationed there. The Irish horse and foot came in great strength down the strand along the riverside. Governor Baker directed the defence and the

---

*I have not followed events in Enniskillen during the siege of Londonderry in any detail for two reasons: first, because this is primarily a book about Londonderry and second, because the Irish forces concentrated their energies on Londonderry and very largely ignored Enniskillen, which was at this period no more than a small village. The Irish army's principal concern was to prevent the men from Enniskillen from joining up with the Londonderry men; the chief activities by the Enniskillen men were sallies to harass the Irish army and relieve some of the pressure on Londonderry.

defenders placed their men in three ranks to enable them to maintain a constant fire at the enemy. In the first rush by the Jacobite horse, the horsemen were protected by their armour, but the besieged, noting this, switched their fire to the horses and began to kill them under their riders. The accounts of this affair — like the accounts of all the actions during this period of the siege — are extremely confused, but Walker estimates that the besiegers lost 400 in the battle, and Ash says that besides those killed or taken prisoner, there were at least 120 wounded. The casualties of the besieged once again seem to have been extremely light — one estimate puts it as low as six privates and one officer.

Plunkett* admits that at least 200 men were lost without doing any damage to the defenders. 'You see here,' he adds, 'as you have seen all along, that the tradesmen of Londonderry have more skill in their defence than the great officers of the Irish army in their attacks.'

---

*In a manuscript *Light to the Blind*, dated 1711 in the collection of Lord Fingal; the author is believed to be Nicholas Plunkett, an eminent lawyer who was a zealous Catholic and an enemy of England. It is widely believed that the anonymous *A Jacobite Narrative of the War in Ireland, 1688 – 91*, published in Dublin in 1892, is based on this manuscript.

IX *Brass money and wooden shoes*

Having failed in their first attempts to bombard the city into surrender, the besiegers now decided to blockade it and to starve the citizens into surrender.

Londonderry stands on a striking site, an oblong hill about 100 feet high, overlooking the River Foyle about four miles from its mouth in the Lough of the same name. In those days it had walls about twenty-four feet high and eight or nine feet thick, with a ditch outside – empty, as already mentioned, in most places, with a couple of drawbridges over it – flanked by nine bastions and two half-bastions. Inside this fortress town there were 7,000 well-armed and determined soldiers, mostly amateur, as well as a considerable body of townspeople and refugees from the surrounding countryside.

Belloc says: 'Why such a blockade was ever allowed to be established by so weak a hostile body, why so large a number of trained and well-armed men with such a superiority of guns should have been contained by an insufficient force is still a mystery. But contained they did allow themselves to be and therefore in the long run were pressed for food. Still they always had plenty of powder and shot.'

The conditions, he says, were quite unsuitable for a siege, or even a blockade. The total royal force on paper was 13,000 but the number of these that could be spared for the assault on Londonderry was not above 6,000. There had been days of incessant rain through which these raw troops had marched; there was no proper surgical or medical equipment, no doctors, no medicines, no surgeons. Enniskillen lay on the flank and called for the attention of whatever other troops were available. 'If we try to put the thing on military terms,' Belloc goes on, 'it is almost farcical; a larger, better-equipped force contained behind its walls by a smaller and worse-equipped one, a formidable defensive attacked with inferior weapons that could not affect it: the besiegers working at a great distance from their ultimate base, over very bad roads, the besieged handicapped by no distance over which to convey their munitions and arms, living under conditions of comfort so long as the provisions lasted, the besiegers in the open field under what was, at the beginning of the operations, abominable weather. I have said that it is a mystery how, under these conditions, the men of Derry allowed themselves to be shut up at all. If the mystery can be solved, it can doubtfully be so from the different command on the two sides. The King's army was led by officers experienced in European warfare; the regular commanders of the rebel [Protestant] side had abandoned action and the men of Derry were led by amateurs of whom the most famous was Mr Walker, a clergyman, a rector from Co. Tyrone ... he at least had no doubt that the war was a war of religion!'

Left to their own judgement, Belloc says, trained professional officers would not have attempted to reduce Londonderry. Rosen, the man in chief command, knew very well that the idea of a siege was nonsense and objected to it from the very beginning.

Theoretically, the person who ordered the operation was King James himself, but James acted on the advice of Melfort, his Secretary of State for Ireland, who was interested in securing Londonderry as a base for the invasion of Scotland and not on any other considerations. Hamilton, who was in charge of operations before Londonderry, had already reported to Dublin that only one musket in ten could be expected to work properly. 'It sounds ridiculous,' Belloc adds, 'but I believe it to be historically true that for effective purposes the Royal Infantry in front of Derry in the first weeks of the siege could not have counted on at the most more than 3,000 in the actual line, and that the useful firearms at their disposal were certainly less than 400.'

It is obvious, he goes on, that in such conditions the besiegers must dig themselves in, or they would be at the mercy of surprise sallies by the numerous and well-armed besieged. But there were only thirty shovels available for the rapid entrenchment of 3,000 men.

A contemporary Jacobite account of the war is equally scathing about the conduct of the siege. It is *A Jacobite Narrative of the War in Ireland, 1688–91*, edited by John T. Gilbert and published in Dublin in 1892. The anonymous writer* says:

> You might think that the besieging army would have made up its mind how it was going to go about reducing the city, whether by making a breach in the wall, or by undermining the same, or by a scalade, or by reducing the garrison to misery by bombs and fireworks, or by famishing it. Londonderry is situated on the banks of a river which mixes thereabouts with the sea, flowing in a narrow channel between two lands. The town is defended on the one side by the said river. On the other side, it has no outer works of any moment. The wall is thick and well lined with a rampart. However, one part of it may soon be battered with the proper cannon. Scaling the walls thereof is practicable for it was that way taken in the wars of Oliver Cromwell. The town is small and therefore it may be rendered uninhabitable by half a dozen large mortars playing constantly for a week.

The writer then goes on to consider the lack of battering pieces in the Irish army, referring to eight cannon, two of them 18-pounders, the remainder 'petty guns'. These produced little effect because they were fired not *at* the wall but *over* it, amongst the houses. Of mortars, there were only two, one large and one small. The larger one very quickly went out of action, so that M. Pointis, the French expert, had little opportunity to display his skill at bombardment. Why were other mortars not brought to Derry, the anonymous author asks, since there was at the time 'gross artillery' in other parts of the Kingdom, and since mortars might have been cast in Dublin, or sent from France? If this was not done, why was the siege attempted? At least, why was it carried on? Some say that the design was to famish the town. But if so, and this appears to have been the final resolution,

---

*Probably Nicholas Plunkett. See p. 127.

why were the besiegers exposed to danger, first by having no lines of defence for the greater part of the duration of the siege, and secondly by sending the men upon attacks in extraordinary disadvantage, 'as in the day advanced and against enemies covered altogether with defence'? For, he says, 'the famishment might just as easily have been procured by keeping the army at a distance, or in good trenches, so that the town could only be relieved with provisions by sea.'

He then goes on to ask why, if the taking of the town depended upon stopping a single ship from coming up the Foyle to the city, far more rigorous measures were not taken to render the river unnavigable at this point. It is true that the fort at Culmore was in the hands of the Irish army, but cannon fire from a fortress on the shore could not in those days stop a ship from passing. The writer of the *Jacobite Narrative* argues very cogently that the task of preventing a ship from coming up the river could far more easily have been done by sinking a couple of gabards – barges – in the roads. This was proposed to General Hamilton but he would not do it on the grounds that it would afterwards destroy the commerce of Londonderry and thereby reduce the Royal revenue. It is said that he had the King's authority for this decision, but the Jacobite author argues that even if this were true, it would have been better to suffer a small detriment than a major disaster. In any case, he is not satisfied that it *is* true; he argues further that the commerce of the town would not necessarily be destroyed by sinking barges in the roads because the bar was merely three miles away from the town, and goods carried by ships stopped by the sunken gabards could easily be carried the rest of the way into the town by barge, a situation which would not only have solved the problem but would also have provided a good livelihood for many in the town. Furthermore, he argues that even if gabards were sunk at the bar, they could easily be taken up later and the river cleared because the river at this point is shallow at low tide.

Among his other criticisms of the conduct of the war, the writer of the *Jacobite Narrative* has this to say:

Besides the neglect committed by the Irish Catholic managers of the King's War in Ireland and by others who had a hand therein, vice reigned amongst them at that very juncture. Stealth in the commonality was unsupportable, which certainly drew down from Heaven the greatest vengeance on the nation, and drinking, gaming, swearing, insulting, indevotion, envy, pride and lasciviousness in many of the officers of the Army, and treachery in some few as it was suspected and covetuousness and dishonest dealing in several of the civil officers, upon which some curious persons, reflecting as they passed their judgement that the King and his Loyalists would be losers, as at last it happened.

Although General Hamilton would not allow barges to be sunk at the bar of the River Foyle just above the town, he did agree that a boom should be erected across the river near Culmore fort, as a barrier to prevent ships from reaching Londonderry from the sea. A row of stakes was driven into the river bed, and a series of large baulks of timber, bound together by ropes and chains, formed a boom more than a quarter of a mile in length, firmly fastened to the shore on each side by cable.

All the entrances to the city were thus closed and every precaution was taken against the introduction of new supplies overland. In addition to the boom, the banks on each side of the river were fringed with forts and batteries — some armed with cannon which had recently arrived from France — to hinder the passage of any ships attempting to get up the river to relieve the beleaguered city.

The second stage in the siege of Derry had now begun.

Meanwhile, King James was holding court in Dublin. On his return to the capital city he heard that a French fleet had anchored in Bantry Bay, an inlet in south-west Cork near Killarney, and had there landed a large stock of military stores and money. But the British Admiral Herbert, who had been sent to intercept the French fleet, had heard that the French were in Bantry Bay and had sailed into the Bay intending to give battle to them. The winds had proved unfavourable, the French force was superior, and after firing a few salvoes Herbert stood out to sea again, and then sailed off to the Scillies looking for reinforcements. While he was away, the French fleet sailed out of Bantry Bay and made its way back to Brest.

Both sides elected to regard this inconclusive encounter as a victory. Westminster passed a vote of thanks to Herbert; and James — who as a former Admiral of the British Fleet was secretly proud of Herbert's boldness in attempting to attack a superior French Fleet in Bantry Bay and could not altogether conceal this pride — nevertheless ordered bonfires to be lighted and a *Te Deum* to be sung in honour of the French victory.

On the day after the celebrations of this futile engagement, a parliament assembled in Dublin. Of the hundred-odd peers summoned, only fourteen turned up, and ten of these were Catholics. The Protestant Bishops of Meath, Ossory, Cork and Limerick also put in an appearance — perhaps to keep their end up, perhaps for fear of some sort of reprisals if they failed to attend — and seventeen new peers were created, all of them Catholics.

The House of Commons consisted almost entirely of Irish Catholics. About 250 members took their seats, of whom only six were Protestants. With few exceptions they were, in the nature of things, men without any experience of the legislature. They had never sat in the House of Commons before. They had never even taken an active part in an election. Because of their religion, they had not been magistrates nor had they served on juries; in fact, they had no experience whatever of public affairs. 'The English squire of that age,' Macaulay says, 'though assuredly not a very profound or enlightened politician, was a statesman and a philosopher when compared with the Roman Catholic squire of Munster or Connaught.' Prejudice certainly, but probably true.

The parliaments of Ireland at this time had no fixed place of assembly. Indeed they met so seldom and usually broke up so speedily that it would hardly have been worth building a regular meeting place for them. On this occasion they met in a building roughly on the site of the present Four Courts in Dublin. It had once been a monastery of Dominican Friars but since the Reformation had been appropriated by the legal profession and was known at this period as the King's Inns.

On 7 May, dressed in his Royal robes and wearing a crown, James took his seat in the House of Lords and summoned the Commons. He expressed his gratitude to the people of Ireland for standing by him when the rest of his realm had deserted him, the rightful ruler; and then he firmly declared once again his determination to abolish all religious inequalities. He acknowledged his debt to the King of France and invited both houses to consider the problems created by the Acts of Settlement and to think about ways in which the original owners of the confiscated lands could best be compensated.

The Commons then appointed Sir Richard Nagle, Attorney General, as speaker, and the debates began. Speaker after speaker dwelt at length on his own adversities and clamoured for the restoration of his former estates in full, ranting about the wrongs that had been done to him at such length and in such detail that Judge Daly complained that these gentlemen were a rabble and not a true parliament and that they resembled fishermen and market gardeners more than politicians. These remarks were conveyed to the Commons and there might have been trouble but for the fact that word now reached the House that Londonderry had fallen at last. There was wild rejoicing, and Daly's insult was overlooked in the enthusiasm. In a few hours time it was known that Londonderry was still holding out as stubbornly as ever, but by now attention had been diverted from Daly to other, more pressing matters.

An Act granting complete liberty of conscience to all Christian sects was next passed. This was followed by the introduction of a Bill annulling the authority of the English Parliament to act as the supreme legislature.

Next the confiscations of land started. The personal estates of all absentees over seventeen years of age were first transferred to the Stuart Crown. A Bill repealing the Acts of Settlement and transferring many thousands of square miles of land from the Cromwellian settlers to the original landlords was greeted with acclamation. The problems inherent in this piece of legislation are obvious though it is easy enough to understand what prompted the Irish MPs to urge it on the King. Even Macaulay, who never had much use for the Irish, is bound to admit that they had a point here.

> Of legislation such as this it is impossible to speak too severely, but for the legislators there are excuses which it is the duty of the historian to notice. They acted unmercifully, unjustly, unwisely. But it would be absurd to expect mercy, justice or wisdom from a class of men first abased by many years of oppression and then maddened by the joy of a sudden deliverance, and armed with irresistible power. The representatives of the Irish nation . . . had lived in a state of constant irritation. With aristocratical sentiments, they had been in a servile position. With the highest pride of blood, they had been exposed to daily affronts, such as might have roused the choler of the humblest plebeian. In sight of the fields and castles which they regarded as their own, they had been glad to be invited by a peasant to partake of his whey and potatoes. Those violent emotions of hatred and cupidity which the situation of the native gentleman could scarcely fail to call forth, appeared to him under the specious guise of patriotism and piety. For his enemies were the enemies of his nation; and the same tyranny which had robbed him of his patrimony had robbed his Church of vast wealth bestowed upon her by the devotion of an earlier age. How was power likely to be used by an uneducated and inexperienced man, agitated by strong desires and resentments which he mistook for sacred duties? And, when two or three hundred such men were brought together in one assembly, what was to be expected but that the passions which each had long nursed in silence would be at once matured into fearful vigour by the influence of sympathy?

Between James and his Parliament, there was little in common other than a hatred of the Protestant religion. The few Irish Protestants who still adhered to him and the British nobles who had followed him into exile and had accompanied him to Ireland from France, attempted to persuade him that it was utter folly to try to repeal these Settlement Acts. They argued that the military adventurers to whom Cromwell had given the Irish land in the first place might well be regarded as wrong-doers and not entitled to it, but how much of it had since passed, by perfectly legitimate means, into other, totally innocent hands? Was the original injustice, they asked, likely to be corrected by another, even greater injustice? On a more practical basis, they urged him to consider what the effect of this measure was likely to be upon thousands of English families who would face ruin as a result of the repeal of these acts. They pointed out that no English Parliament would ever stand over such legislature, and that if he ever succeeded in getting back to Westminster there would be such a clamour over his action in this matter that he would either have to go into exile again, or go back on his promises to the Irish and reverse the legislation yet again.

James felt that these arguments were unanswerable, as indeed they were. He had several conferences with leading members of the House of Commons and recommended moderation, but they wouldn't listen. It was nonsense, they said, to talk about the rights of the subsequent purchasers of these lands when the land had in fact been stolen from the Irish landlords; how could a right spring out of an initial wrong? People who elected to buy property acquired as the result of a basic injustice had only themselves to blame and must take the consequences of their own folly and greed. Despairing of ever making them see sense, James threatened to dissolve Parliament, but it was soon made very clear to him that if he didn't give the Irish landlords their former lands back, they would not help him to fight to recover his own kingdom.

James next decided to see whether the House of Lords could reason with the Commons and persuade them of the utter impracticability of repealing the Acts of Settlement, or at least put some sort of a check on their activities. In the corridor, he met the Count d'Avaux who was anxious that the measure should go through, because it would mean a final and irreparable breach between England and Ireland, which could be exploited to France's advantage. As a result of Avaux's pressure, James did not openly oppose the repeal of the Acts of Settlement though he still secretly hoped that the Lords would block it, or at least modify it substantially.

The fact that James had yielded to the will of the Commons in the end in not opposing the repeal of the Acts of Settlement cut very little ice with the members of Parliament who regarded him as now having shown his hand as an Englishman at heart, more interested in what Westminster might feel than what was happening in Ireland. One party was for dismissing Melfort, the King's adviser, as an enemy of the nation; another faction wanted to depose all Protestant Bishops, including the four presently sitting in the House of Lords. It was with the great difficulty that Avaux and Tyrconnel restrained the unruly element in the Commons.

Although, eventually, James gave his reluctant assent to the Bill, which would have meant the reconfiscation of all lands held by the Cromwellian settlers since 1641, it never came into effect and the confiscations were not carried out for the reason that King James himself was defeated before the machinery could be put in motion to implement it. This 'Patriot Parliament' as it was called was later held to be illegal and all documents and records connected with it were destroyed.

James had another very serious problem with which to contend. The receipts from the Customs and Excise had dropped by nearly one half. This is not really surprising, in view of the state of the nation. Trade had virtually ceased to exist. Some of the wealthiest and most industrious of the Protestants had emigrated, taking their wealth with them. Much of the fixed capital had been destroyed and a great deal of the remainder was lying idle and unproductive. Thousands of the most industrious of the workers had fled to England and Scotland, or were ensconced in Londonderry or Enniskillen. Most of the more substantial Irish Catholics were serving with King James's army, and had for all practical purposes ceased production. Thousands of head of cattle — the principal wealth of the agricultural parts of the country — had been slaughtered by the Irish. The poverty of the Exchequer was no more than a reflection of the poverty of the nation, and the only effective way either could be restored would be with a period of peace and prosperity. James was desperately short of money with which to conduct the war. The Commons voted him £20,000 a month, to be levied on real estate, but in a country at war there was no effective way of collecting this money.

James now had the idea that he could extricate himself from all his financial difficulties by a form of devaluation – a solution to which desperate governments have resorted in much more recent times. With the horror which all decent Victorians felt at any deviation from the gold standard, Macaulay describes this ploy as 'coining false money' and 'calling a farthing a shilling'. Pots, pans, door-knockers, old weapons and ornaments were carried to the mint, he reports, melted down and turned into base coinage. In a short time base money to the nominal value of £1,000,000 – over £8,000,000 in today's terms – was in circulation and a Royal edict had declared that these base coins were legal tender in all cases. Thus, Macaulay goes on indignantly, a mortgage of £1,000 could be cleared off by a bag of counters made out of old kettles. And the tradesmen of Dublin, who were mostly Protestants, were the chief losers. The magistrates made it obligatory on them to accept the new coinage, so that a man might walk into a shop, lay down a piece of brass worth threepence, and carry off goods worth half a guinea. Soldiers patrolled the shops to see that the new law was everywhere being obeyed, and traders who refused to accept the new coins were jailed. A great deal of the Protestant mistrust of Catholic business methods stems from this affair and to this day the standard toast of the Loyal Orange Lodges contains the line: 'To the glorious, pious and immortal memory of King William III, who saved us from rogues and roguery, slaves and slavery, knaves and knavery, *from brass money and wooden shoes.*' The italics are mine, and 'wooden shoes' is a reference to the French who sometimes wore a form of *sabot*.

In fact, the experiment was a lot more successful than Macaulay allows and worked, up to a point, though it certainly caused massive inflation, until the spring of 1690, when it was common to give forty or fifty shillings in 'brass' money for a genuine guinea. After King James's defeat, understandably, the brass money took a further nose-dive and a base half-crown was worth only about a penny.

The Commons were willing to concede power to King James to create this false currency because it mainly damaged the Protestants. There can be little doubt that the destruction of the Protestant settlers was one of the prime aims of this Parliament, and to this end they now set about trying to get the King's assent to an Act of Attainder.

A list was made containing between two and three thousand names of men who were said to have joined King William's side. At the top of this list was half the peerage in Ireland, many of the baronets, knights, clergymen, squires, merchants and yeomen, and the list even included some women and children. No investigation of these people was ever made. As Macaulay puts it, any member of Parliament who wished to rid himself of a rival, a creditor or even a private enemy, had merely to give the name to the clerk at the table, and in most cases it was added to the list without any further discussion.

Days were next fixed by which those whose names were on the list had to present themselves for trial. If the person attainted was in Ireland, he had to present himself by 10 August of that year, 1689. If he had left Ireland since 5 November 1688, he had to surrender himself by 1 October. If he failed to appear, he was liable to be hanged, drawn and quartered.

Regulations were passed making the use of the Royal prerogative in pardoning people on this list as difficult as possible. Furthermore, the list contained the names of many people who, although Protestants, were fanatical Royalists and had staked everything to support the Stuart succession. One such was Henry Dodwell, a professor in the University of Oxford. But he was a Protestant and he had property in Ireland, and so his name was added to the list. The list was never published, and most of the people who were attainted knew nothing of it. However, as in the case of the repeal of the Acts of Settlement, James did not survive long enough for the measure to be put effectively into practice. Some lands belonging to absentee Williamites were in fact seized and leased out to Irish landlords but the operation ceased when James decided that the officers who were carrying out this duty were more urgently needed to assist him in the conduct of the war.

The news of these laws which were passed during the ten

weeks that the Patriot Parliament sat in Dublin leaked through to the beleaguered cities in the north and did much to steel the inhabitants of Londonderry and Enniskillen in their determination to hold out; also, it did a great deal of damage to King James's cause in England, where there had been some signs of a reaction against the Bloodless Revolution in James's favour which might otherwise have led to a counter-revolution in England. But throughout the whole time that Parliament was sitting, every settler who succeeded in escaping across the Irish Sea to Holyhead or Bristol brought ever more fearsome reports of the tyranny under which the Irish Protestants were groaning.

The fugitive colonists were well treated in Britain where the House of Commons placed £15,000 at King William's disposal for the relief of refugees from Ireland. Commissions in the army were given to those qualified to serve and an Act was passed which enabled clergymen who had lost their offices in Ireland to hold office in England. The Commons also took a great interest in the stories which the settlers brought back of the way in which the Protestants in the north had been holding out. This provoked more than one outburst in the Commons. 'This is no time to be counting cost,' Colonel John Birch, a vociferous MP, exploded on one occasion; 'Are those brave fellows in Londonderry to be deserted? If we lose them, will not the world cry shame upon us? A boom across the river! Why have we not cut the boom in pieces? Are our brethren to perish almost in sight of England, within a few hours voyage of our shores?'

The Commons appointed a committee to inquire into the delays and indecisions which had very nearly proved fatal to the English cause in Northern Ireland. Lundy, as we have already seen, was sent to the Tower and Richards and Cunningham were also arrested. But the anger of the House of Commons was to some extent assuaged by the news that, before the end of summer, an army sufficiently powerful to re-establish the English cause in Ireland would be sent across the Irish Sea under General Count Frederick von Schomberg, whom William had made commander-in-chief of his forces in Ireland, and in the meantime an expedition strong enough to relieve Londonderry would be immediately despatched from

Liverpool under the command of Major-General Percy Kirke.

X   The relief expedition

Meanwhile Londonderry and Enniskillen continued to defend themselves with stubborn courage. The men of Enniskillen in particular never ceased to wage war on their enemies. Early in May they marched out to attack a large body of troops from Connaught who had invaded Donegal. The Irish troops were defeated and fled to Sligo, leaving behind them 120 dead and 60 prisoners. Two pieces of artillery and some horses were captured by the Enniskillen men.

Emboldened by this success, they next invaded Cavan, drove 1,500 of King James's troops before them, captured Ballincarrig, the strongest fort in that part of the kingdom, and carried off all the pikes and muskets of the garrison.

Then they turned to Co. Meath, where they captured 3,000 oxen and 2,000 sheep and carried them off as supplies for their island garrison on Lough Erne.

The news of these exploits reached Dublin and Colonel Hugh Sutherland was ordered to march against Enniskillen with a regiment of dragoons and two battalions of foot. In the usual style, he was carrying arms to distribute among the Irish peasantry *en route*. Once again, instead of waiting for him to come and attack them, the men of Enniskillen sallied out to meet him. He retreated, leaving all his stores at Belturbet, in the care of 300 soldiers. The Protestants from Enniskillen now attacked Belturbet making their way into a tall house which overlooked the town, from which they began to fire on the King's soldiers. Within two hours, the garrison had surrendered. The haul, which consisted of 700 muskets, a great quantity of powder, many horses, some sacks of biscuits and barrels of meal, was eagerly seized and gleefully hauled back to Enniskillen, where the food would keep the garrison fed until the harvest — which was now not far off. Incidentally, throughout the war, the besieged at

Enniskillen continued to till the earth in the immediate vicinity of their strongholds, unlike the native Irish who neglected cultivation as soon as the war broke out, and relied on marauding to bring them food.

On the whole, the men of Enniskillen were more successful in their sallies than the Londonderry garrison, and one of their objectives in making so many sallies was to relieve the pressure on the city. This was done not only out of a feeling of loyalty to their co-religionists there, but also from the knowledge that once Londonderry fell, all the might of King James's forces would be concentrated on them. However, there was not much more that they could do to assist Londonderry other than send out parties to harass and molest the rearguard of the blockading army and drive away any troops which approached too close to their own city walls.

But despite the doughty efforts of the Enniskillen men to relieve the pressure on Londonderry – and on one occasion they managed to carry off all the horses of three entire troops of cavalry who were engaged in besieging the city – it was now tightly surrounded by Irish army posts. The boom was firmly in position across the river, and the river banks were fringed with fortified positions and closely guarded. Food was now definitely running out. As early as 8 June, horseflesh was the only meat available and it was scarce. It had been decided to make up the deficiency with tallow, but even this unpalatable alternative had to be strictly rationed. The tallow was mixed with flour and made into a sort of cake which proved sustaining.

In May, Captain Jacob Richards at Liverpool received orders from Schomberg to embark with four regiments to relieve Londonderry; two days later Major-General Kirke and Colonel Trelawney arrived and preparations were started for victualling the ships for the regiments.

At a council of war called by Kirke, it was decided to send Captain Jacob Richards ahead of the regiments. His instructions were to try to reach Londonderry first, to advise the Protestants there of the measures that were being taken

for their relief, and to make arrangements for the forti-
fication of the town. Accordingly three ships – the frigate
Greyhound, the ketch *Kingfisher* and a merchant ketch, the
Edward and James – left Liverpool for Lough Foyle with a
lieutenant and ensign and forty men on board, including
some gunners and mining experts.

Their instructions were that they were to go no further
than Culmore fort; they were to stay above the fort until
they had received information about the state of
Londonderry, whether batteries were in position and whether
the channel was choked or obstructed in any way to prevent
the passage of ships. They were not to continue the journey
to the city if there was any danger of losing the ships, but
instead were to report back to Kirke.

The three ships duly arrived in Lough Foyle and anchored
off Culmore fort on 7 June. Richards observed the boom
from his maintop and decided that his ships were not
powerful enough to force it. As the frigate *Greyhound* was
weighing anchor to return and report this information to
Kirke, she ran aground and was immediately fired on by the
Irish batteries. More than fifty shots were fired against her
hull and upperworks, and at one period it was seriously
considered abandoning her and setting her on fire, but a
lucky shift in the wind blew her off the shore and she was
able to limp back to Scotland for a refit.

When Hamilton learned that three English ships had been
up the Foyle, he realized it was only a matter of time until
they returned in greater strength and decided to redouble his
efforts to prevent any ships from getting through to the city.
He still resolutely refused to allow any barges to be sunk in
the roads, but the boom was rebuilt and strengthened.

There are considerable discrepancies in the references to
the building of the boom. Mackenzie says it was built *after*
Kirke's ships were seen in the Foyle but other accounts
specifically mention that Richards observed the boom from
his maintop and decided that it would be too strong to force.
Pointis, who was responsible for the engineering work in
connection with the boom, reports on its completion after
news had been received that troops had been embarked at
Liverpool for the relief of Londonderry.

Some of the confusion probably results from the fact that there was not one boom but two, or possibly even three. The first one was made of timber, joined by iron chains and fortified by a cable twisted around it, but because the timber chosen was oak, it would not float and soon broke up. The besiegers then apparently built one of fir, which answered the purpose better, though there are some accounts to the effect that this boom was carried away by the tide. Then there is a detailed account in a report by Pointis of a boom made out of beams removed from houses in the area. These beams were a foot square in thickness and were joined to each other by mortise joints of a foot and a half. Each beam end was attached to the next by iron cramps, leaving a certain amount of play. Placed crosswise and under the mortises was one end of a cable – iron and chain were not available, Pointis says – doubled and well fixed through each beam. Running through the whole boom was a five- or six-inch rope, the thickest that Pointis could lay his hands upon. This was joined to the beams by the iron cramps through which it ran like a rod in curtain rings.

This make-shift contraption was fastened at one end to a bridge, according to some accounts, and at the other to a piece of timber forced into the ground and fortified with a piece of stonework. It could not have resisted any determined assault upon it, though its presence across the river could delay ships within range of the Irish cannon on the shore.

Also, on the left bank of the river, where it rises in a steep slope, Pointis had entrenchments dug in the form of an amphitheatre, where the Irish soldiers would be safe even from artillery. Pointis believed that the relieving forces would not attempt to cut through the boom with hatchets or swords because in order to do this they would need to come within pistol shot of this entrenchment. He was so pleased with his handiwork, and so convinced of its effectiveness, that he could hardly wait for the relieving forces to reach Londonderry and prove him right.

Pointis also had plans to build a second boom further up the river nearer to Londonderry, but although he repeatedly refers to this second stockade in his letters to Louis, he seems never to have got around to building it. The theory behind

Pointis's thinking was that in order to break the boom, the British ships would have to have the wind dead aft of them. But with the wind from this quarter they would be pinned against the boom with no chance of escape, if the boom failed to yield; and thus pinned they would be at the mercy of the Jacobite guns. The presence of the entrenchment would theoretically prevent the ships from sending their sailors in longboats to attack the boom with axes.

Nevill, who examined the boom after the siege, reports that it was about 200 yards long and five or six feet wide. It was, he says, fixed to a frame in the rock at the western end, and to a frame at the eastern end fixed under a great heap of stones. It floated with the tides and spanned only the deep-water channel.

Kirke did not arrive in Lough Foyle with the main fleet – about thirty ships in all, of varying sizes – until 11 June. Some of the ships had been forced back by the wind and had to put into Ramsey Bay on the Isle of Man. Captain John Leake, in charge of the frigate *Dartmouth*, picked up a victualler in Ramsey Bay and was forced into Rathlin Island where he took advantage of the situation by collecting a hundred head of cattle.

George Rooke, who was in charge of the fleet, ordered Captain Leake with the *Dartmouth, Greyhound* and *Kingfisher* to join Kirke – since these ships, the smallest in the fleet, were the most suitable to go up-river. Rooke on the *Deptford*, with the *Bonaventura, Portland* and *Antelope*, all frigates, lay off the mouth of the Lough in readiness to give Kirke any assistance he might require and to secure him from attacks on the seaward side.

On the evening of 15 June, Leake arrived in Lough Foyle and the following day, when Kirke's ships were off Greencastle, sailed the *Dartmouth* to within a mile of Culmore and anchored there. On the same day, 15 June, two further ships laden with provisions were sent from Glasgow under the escort of the frigate *Jersey*.

The ships had been sighted from the besieged town and there was great rejoicing. Signals were made from the spires and steeples and returned from the mastheads in the bay, but in the absence of any prearranged code, these signals were meaningless to both sides.

Now the mood of indecision and apathy which had gripped Lundy seemed to take hold of Major-General Kirke and for the next few weeks he behaved in what appears to be a most inexplicable and illogical fashion. On the evening of Sunday 16 June, he consulted the pilots of the fleet to see whether any of them would undertake the piloting of the *Swallow* or any of the smaller ships right up to the city of Londonderry. There was a lot of talk but nothing positive seems to have emerged, though several of the pilots believed it to be possible to get through to Londonderry. There were discussions as to whether the boom could in fact be broken, and speculation as to whether there might be barges in the roads; after a further council of war a few days later, attended by all the colonels, lieutenant-colonels and naval captains, Kirke seemed satisfied that it would be impracticable to force a passage through to Londonderry.

The council decided instead to hold its hand until the relieving forces had been augmented and then try to reach the city overland. They were convinced, in view of the length of time that Richards had already been in the Foyle, and the time that the fleet had been there, that the very fact that no message had reached them from the inhabitants of the city could be taken as an indication that they were not yet hard pressed either by the enemy or by a shortage of food. It didn't seem to have occurred to anybody at the council that the reason why there was no message was simply that there was no longer any way by which the hard-pressed inhabitants of Londonderry could get a message out to the fleet; nor did it occur to anybody that, if they could, the inhabitants would have got a message out to the fleet, whatever its content.

That evening Kirke went aboard the *Dartmouth*. As this was the advance ship Captain Richards was posted to observe what the enemy was doing. From his maintop he could easily see the boom across the river.

The besieged now lit a beacon on the steeple of the cathedral as a sign of their distress, but the relieving force did not know what construction to put on this bonfire, and so they ignored it.

The Irish army had reacted in its own way to the arrival of the British ships. At the first sight of them, the Irish started to pull down their tents and desert in droves, but when after a few days the ships didn't seem to be making any attempt to relieve the city, or to behave in any way belligerently towards the troops on the river banks, they started to steal back again, drawing their cannon down to the edge of the river.

In desperation, the inhabitants of Londonderry built a boat of about eight oars a side, to try to get the news of their plight down to the fleet, but it was forced back by heavy fire.

By 16 June, there were more than thirty ships lying between Culmore fort and the mouth of the Lough. The besieged fired their cannon from the walls and steeple three times, and the cannon on the ships replied but again, as there was no pre-arranged code, no communication was achieved.

The elation which the besieged had felt at the sight of the ships in the lough now turned to misery. Kirke withdrew to the mouth of the lough where he lay totally inactive, or so it seemed to the besieged, for many weeks, in full sight of the starving city.

By now the pressure of famine was becoming intense. Strict house-to-house searches were made to ensure that nobody was hiding stores of food or concealing provisions belonging to people who had died or had deserted the town. The stock of cannon balls was almost exhausted and the besieged were using substitutes made of brickdust, covered with a thin coating of lead – some accounts have it that they were using bullets made of lead with brick in the centre. Disease had made its appearance in the city, and soon began to take a heavier toll of the inhabitants than ever the enemy's bombs had done; it is reported that fifteen officers died of fever in one day.

One of the most extraordinary features of this extraordinary siege was the fact that Kirke and his reinforcements arrived in the area without having made any arrangements whatsoever for communication with the inhabitants, and never made any organized effort to establish communications. It had been impressed upon Kirke that the matter was urgent and he had already wasted a considerable amount of time as a result of adverse winds and bad weather during the passage. The matter of his dilatoriness was raised in Parliament on 22 June.

We have seen how the besieged attempted to reach the fleet by boat but were driven back by heavy gunfire. Kirke also sent two (unnamed) men in a half-hearted attempt to get through the Irish lines to Londonderry but one returned on 22 June having got no further than the Irish camp, where he had been stopped by sentinels. He reported that he had lost his companion the night before, but had heard some talk about the fact that the Papists had taken a spy and had hanged him that morning. This he assumed to be his missing companion, of whom no more seems to have been heard. The hope of establishing contact by sending men from the fleet into the town was not, however, abandoned and two more men, James Roche – who had been wounded in the Bantry Bay adventure – and James Cromie, a Scot, were selected to make an attempt to reach the city.

Roche was landed by boat at a place called Faughan on 23 June. James's army was encamped in the area, but Roche managed to get through the lines safely, covering eight miles in the dead of night, until he reached the Fish House, three miles beyond Londonderry, where he entered the water and swam to the city. As he didn't have any identification papers or letters of credit, he was taken for a spy and was in grave danger of being executed until he managed to persuade the garrison to allow him to go up into the cathedral steeple and make signs to the fleet which would be acknowledged by Kirke according to a pre-arranged pattern – the first piece of intelligent thinking in this whole affair.

When the answers came back, exactly as Roche had predicted they would, he was accepted for what he was. The garrison then told him that they had not provisions to last for more than four or five days at the most, and implored him to bring them speedy relief. Roche, exhausted as he was, undertook to swim back to the Fish House. By now it was about one o'clock in the morning. As he went ashore, he was seen by a party of Irish dragoons and, pursued by them, he fled naked through the bog and had to leap from a rock thirty feet high into the water again. He was fired on and wounded at least three times – some accounts say five times – but managed to swim back to Londonderry, arriving there at about 4 a.m. on 25 June. There he remained for several days, attempting to convey information about the state of the city from the steeple, but it seems that no provision had been made for the exchange of any information other than the bare news that he had arrived safely in the city and consequently his attempts to communicate were no more successful than the townspeople's own earlier attempts had been. According to a letter he wrote to the House of Commons later, when he was trying to get some sort of recognition for his signal services, he had, in the course of a few hours on the night of 24–25 June, walked about eight miles, swam nine miles, run three miles naked and had been wounded five times.

There are discrepancies in this story. Roche says he landed on Monday 23 June, but 23 June was in fact a Sunday. Richards's diary says that Roche was put ashore on Tuesday 25 June. Roche apparently gave the garrison full details of the ships, men and provisions which had been sent for the relief of the town, and mentioned to them that there were thirty ships below Culmore and more expected shortly.

The other messenger of the fleet, the Scot James Cromie, got as far as Newbuildings, opposite the town. As he couldn't swim, he lay there hidden waiting for a boat to be sent to fetch him, as Roche had promised to arrange. Whether Roche forgot all about the boat in the excitement of all the comings and goings of that eventful night is not known, but no boat ever arrived for Cromie and on Thursday, 27 June, the besieging army found him, took him prisoner and carried him to the Jacobite camp in Strong's Orchard. He was very frightened and after some close interrogation agreed to give the besieged a completely inaccurate account of the relief expedition. The Jacobites then hoisted a white flag and invited the Protestants to parley with Cromie whom they had captured and who, they said, would tell the besieged that all was confusion within the fleet.

Accordingly, a party under Lieutenant-Colonel Blair and Lieutenant-Colonel Fortescue was sent across the river to hear what Cromie had to say. It didn't take them long to discover what Cromie was at and when Lieutenant Colonel Blair asked him how it was that he gave such a different account of the fleet from that furnished by Roche, Cromie replied truthfully enough that he was a prisoner in Jacobite hands whereas Roche was safe and sound behind Londonderry's walls. There seem to have been some half-hearted attempts to exchange Cromie for other prisoners but nothing came of them and Cromie remained a prisoner in the Jacobite camp.

Meanwhile, the return of Roche and Cromie was being eagerly awaited in the fleet. Cromie had told the Jacobites of the arrangements that had been made for them to rejoin the fleet with the result that when the boat which was sent to pick him up approached within a pistol shot of the shore it was fired upon by the Irish army.

Roche continued with his ineffectual attempts to convey information to the fleet from the steeple of the cathedral.

A man called McGimpsey now went to Colonel Murray and offered to try to swim out to the fleet. Murray gave McGimpsey a message to carry with him. It was concealed in a small bladder, tied around his neck, and weighted with two musket balls on the theory that if he happened to fall into enemy hands, he could break the string and allow the weighted bladder to sink. McGimpsey started off about ten o'clock on the night of 26 June from Shipquay, and before long was drowned. His body was recovered by the Irish army, though the garrison did not know this of course, and when he was taken out of the water, it was found that he was still wearing the bladder tied around his neck. It contained not one letter but three, one of which, signed by Walker, Baker and Michelburne, read as follows: 'We have endeavoured to send you several expresses but could not get it done. If this reaches your hands let us hear from you by him, and what succours we may expect from England, and how soon, and if he gets thither this night, hang up your flags on the maintop and fire some guns at the hour of eleven in the morning which may be a signal to us of his arrival with you . . . '

The writers go on to give a brief account of the situation in and around Londonderry, and tell of the effect of the arrival of the fleet on the besiegers who took down their tents, removed their mortars, bombs and artillery and sent away their sick and wounded. Then, seeing that the forces of the fleet had made no attempt to land, they took courage again. brought back the things which they had removed and laid close siege to the city again. The letter mentions that provisions, horseflesh included, would not last above eight or ten days. The writers ask Kirke to send in a small vessel or two laden with provisions of any kind, but especially request that a good part of the provisions should be biscuits, cheese and butter, 'because there was no firing left to dress meat'. The letter expressed the belief that the ships could come to the quays without hazard. In a post-script the writers say that they will answer with the garrison's guns on the church steeple and add: 'If you do not send us relief we must surrender the garrison within six or seven days.'

Kirke never saw this letter. Instead of reaching the fleet the three letters fell into the hands of Rosen who had just arrived in the area to take over the direction of the siege.

XI   *Protestants under the walls*

When, by early June, King James saw that the Irish army was making no headway towards reducing the city, he ordered Rosen, his commander-in-chief, to go north to expedite matters.

Rosen had got about as far as Cavan when he heard of the arrival of the relief ships in Lough Foyle. James now sent a fresh set of instructions to Rosen, on whom he conferred the rank of Marshal-General: Rosen was to march with all speed to Londonderry so that he could support Lieutenant-General Richard Hamilton by giving him some of his troops, or he could take over the command of the siege himself, whichever Rosen preferred. The Marshal-General arrived in the Irish camp on 17 June. On the way up he had complained continually about the bad roads, the lack of arms and the frequent desertions from his forces. He wrote to James that his troops and Hamilton's were few in number, oppressed with fatigue and short of arms and reminded James gently that he had foreseen all this and had warned him against attempting the siege with such a small, ill-armed body of men.

The discrepancy between the armies doesn't seem excessive — despite varied accounts there is overall agreement that at any given moment during the earlier stages of the siege there were about 7,000 armed men inside the walls of Derry and between 6,000 and 10,000 men before the city. But as Sir Charles Petrie points out in his book, *The Jacobite Movement*, no less a soldier than Napoleon himself laid it down that to be successful a besieging army should be four times the strength of the garrison it is attacking.

On his arrival in the camp, Rosen announced that he had decided to leave Hamilton in charge of the siege and concentrate his own energies on preventing the relief forces from reaching the town. Rosen swore that he would demolish the city and bury its inhabitants in its ashes. 'But,' retorts Walker, 'those threatenings as well as his promises, in which he was very eloquent and obliging, had very little power with us, God having under all our difficulties established us with a spirit of resolution, we having devoted our lives to the defence of our city, our religion and the interest of King William and Queen Mary.' However, the spirit of resolution was not all that universal in Derry, for Walker reports, almost in the same breath, that there were desertions from the garrison every day, so that the enemy received constant intelligence of what was going on in the town, to such an extent in fact that the location of the ammunition had to be constantly changed and Walker himself made it a crime, punishable by death, even to discuss the possibility of surrendering.

Despite his announcement that he was going to concentrate on preventing relief from reaching the town, Rosen seemed to concern himself far more with reducing it and was soon ordering mortars and other pieces of ordnance to be placed against the Windmill side of the town and two culverins opposite the Butcher's Gate. The besiegers also now ran a trench up Bog Street to within fifty yards of the Gunner's Bastion, preparatory to laying a mine there.

The besieged counter-mined the enemy camp at Butcher's Gate and raised a blind there to defend it from the enemy's battering guns, after the latter had already done some damage.

The besiegers now tried yet another peace offer to the garrison, promising that if they surrendered the town and laid down their arms they would have a free pardon and liberty to return to their homes, plus compensation for any losses they had suffered. The garrison yet again rejected the offer. This is revealed in one of the three letters found on the swimmer McGimpsey when he was drowned. Walker in a letter to Kirke says that if the besieged did not receive speedy supplies, within a few days, they feared they would have to accept worse conditions than those now being offered. If, however, provisions were sent by the fleet, the besieged would hold out, and he warns Kirke that if the besieged should be forced to yield for want of provisions, it would not be their fault.

The third letter, from Murray, which was also signed by John Cairnes, told Kirke that through lack of provisions the garrison had been eating horseflesh for some time past, and that was now likely to fail too, that great sickness and mortality had been occasioned in the city for want of food and that the people and garrison were 'weakened exceedingly thereby'. Echoing Walker's doubts about the steadfastness of some of the city's defenders, they reported that some 'treacherous men' were running daily to the enemy with their arms, while others were 'treating and tampering with them clandestinely and none of these of the meanest station here, and we know what sad effects their so doing may have on the poor honest men that desire to defend this place and oppose Popery with the hazard of all that is dear to them in the world'. They therefore besought Kirke to 'hasten the city's relief with provisions at least'. Adding that the enemy were drawing ever closer with their trenches, the three signatories declared: 'Our case calls for help, help, help from God and you.'

Rosen, having learnt a great deal about the state of the city from these letters, and about the disposition of the fleet from Cromie, sent to James asking for more reinforcements to be sent and repeating his request that protections should not be granted to persons coming out of the besieged town. His argument was that if the town were completely sealed off, the garrison would have that many more mouths to feed 'by which means they would sooner consume their provisions and be obliged to surrender themselves with a halter about their necks'.

On the day that McGimpsey was drowned attempting to carry the letters from the town to the fleet, a Colonel G. O'Neill of the Irish army asked to have a conference with some of the officers of the garrison. The garrison sent Colonel Lance and Lieutenant-Colonel Campbell to meet him on the strand. Colonel O'Neill told the garrison officers that King James had sent instructions to Rosen to the effect that if the city would surrender, all those who chose to go back to their former dwellings would be free to do so; that those who were prepared to join King James's army would be entertained without distinction of religion; and that those who wished to go to England or Scotland would be free to do so. An answer to this offer was required by 27 June.

The terms of this offer were similar to those mentioned by Walker in his letter of 26 June to Kirke. On the following day, 27 June, the garrison turned it down.

Hamilton now decided to offer formal written terms to the garrison. One would think that the Irish army would have realized by now that the garrison was not likely to surrender, but both King James and his officers seem to have been convinced that if they kept on offering the garrison generous surrender terms – and most of the offers were extremely generous – it would eventually succumb. Hamilton's offer is dated 27 June and the text betrays an element of jealousy between Hamilton and Rosen. It suggests that negotiations with Colonel O'Neill may have broken down because the garrison entertained some doubts that O'Neill was empowered to carry on such talks, or because the proposals came from Rosen and not from Hamilton himself. There was also the point that whereas O'Neill wanted to discuss the offer with officers representing the garrison, the Londonderry delegates had made it quite plain that the garrison as a whole would have to be consulted. Hamilton emphasized that O'Neill had full power to negotiate with the Governor of Londonderry, that he, Hamilton, had full powers to make these proposals; and that Rosen had no right to meddle with what Hamilton did in relation to the siege, as his responsibility was limited to opposing the British relief forces.

As to his right to negotiate, the besieged could see from the King's Warrant that Hamilton had full power to make terms with them. If they did not think this sufficient, Hamilton was prepared to give them whatever additional security they might demand. Those who held commissions from the Prince of Orange need have no fears; it would be in King James's best interests to take as much care of his Protestant subjects as any others, since he made no distinction of religion. Hamilton added that he desired nothing more than to have these proposals communicated to all the people of Londonderry. All those who desired to continue to live in the town would have protection and total freedom of their goods and religion. Those who wished to return to their former homes would be provided with a guard to accompany them to their respective habitations, as well as victuals for the journey, and they would be restored to all their former possessions, 'with reprisals of cattle from such as had taken them to the mountains'. This last, as C. D. Milligan tartly remarks, is an interesting acknowledgement of the fact that the homes of the Protestants had been plundered by the Irish and their livestock stolen.

These proposals were lobbed into the town encased in a blank bomb. Mackenzie says this was done to ensure that the terms would be widely known and not kept from the garrison and townsfolk. Hamilton imagined that at this stage the townsfolk and soldiers might be far more inclined to accept such generous terms than Governor Walker and some of the leading officers who had become almost fanatical in their determination to resist at all costs.

Walker says that these conditions were offered to the town which by this time was living on horseflesh, dogs, cats, rats and mice, greaves – dregs of melted tallow – starch and salted hides. 'Yet,' says Walker, 'they unanimously resolved to eat the Irish and then one another, rather than surrender to any but their own King William and Queen Mary.'

The city's answer to this offer from Hamilton was that they wondered he should expect them to place any confidence in him, who had so unworthily broken faith with King William, and the Londonderry garrison could not believe that he had learnt any more sincerity in the Irish camp.

While all these negotiations were going on, the garrison suffered another grave loss in the death of Governor Baker. His duties often meant touring the walls in filthy weather and he had contracted many colds; in the middle of June, he caught a violent fever as a result and was forced to keep to his chamber in the Bishop's House. On 21 June, a council of war was held in Colonel Michelburne's house to elect a

Governor to act in Baker's place until such time as he recovered. The council asked Baker's advice and he suggested Colonel Michelburne. The greater part of the council agreed and Michelburne was confirmed Governor. Walker, who always played up his own part in these affairs, states that around 18 June, when Governor Baker was seriously ill, Colonel Michelburne 'was chosen and appointed to assist Governor Walker, that when one commanded in sallies, the other might take care of the town, and if one should fall, the town might not be left without a government and to the hazard of new elections.'

Baker's health improved for a bit, and he was convalescing when he heard that the Irish were planning a very vigorous attack on the town. This was Lord Clancarty's attempt to force his way into the city through the Butcher's Gate. There was an ancient prophecy that when a Clancarty knocked at the gates of Derry, the enchantment of the town would be broken, and Clancarty apparently now decided to put this prophecy to the test.

He came over the bog on the night of 28 June with his regiment and some other detachments. The troops, led by Lieutenant-Colonel Skelton, attacked the outerworks of the Bishop's Gate and gained possession of them, while some of their mining experts entered a cellar under the Gunner's Bastion. As soon as the attack was discovered by the besieged, a party of the garrison soldiers slipped out from the Bishop's Gate and around the walls to the Butcher's Gate, holding their fire until they were right on top of the besiegers. They then 'thundered upon them', to use Walker's words, while those on the Gunner's Bastion opened fire on them with case shot, and others on the wall fired on them with small shot. So effective was the fire, and so determined the counterattack, that Clancarty's men were driven out of the outerworks which they had taken and back across the bog. Walker says that they left their miners and hundreds of their best men in the field, besides several officers and soldiers who died of their wounds later. Ash says that twenty-five or thirty of the besiegers were killed, and estimates that about twice that number were wounded. Only one of the besieged was killed and one wounded.

But there was another important Protestant casualty as a result of this encounter. Governor Baker, considering that it was vital that he should be with his men to encourage them, went out and stayed on the walls all night. The next morning he had a relapse and died a couple of days later, on 30 June.

All of the contemporary writers on the subject are agreed that his death was a great loss to the garrison; even Walker ungrudgingly says that 'his death was a sensible loss to us, and generally lamented, being a valiant person, in all his actions amongst us he shared the greatest honour, courage and conduct.' Colonel Michelburne had had an argument with Baker earlier during the siege which got so far out of hand that they both drew their swords but Michelburne, who was wounded in the encounter, bore Baker no grudge and referred to him as 'our noble, brave Governor'.

Even in the controversies which followed the publication (in the autumn of 1689) of Walker's account of the siege, nobody had anything but praise for Baker, who was buried in one of the vaults of the cathedral. His pall was borne by Governor Walker and Michelburne and others of the leading officers.

After Baker's death, Colonel Michelburne continued to act as joint Governor with Walker, without any formal confirmation in office by the council of war. Walker continues to refer to himself as the Governor, though he and Michelburne signed various documents as joint Governors. There is the same confusion about the relative positions of Walker and Michelburne as there had been earlier between Walker and Baker. Ash refers to the Governors, in the plural, but he also refers to Michelburne as the Governor. According to Michelburne's own petition to the House of Commons in 1689 he was chosen by the garrison as 'Governor and Commander-in-Chief with Dr Walker', he (Colonel Michelburne) 'performing all the duties during all the difficulties of the siege, having all charge of the military part.' When the controversy over Walker's governorship arose, certificates were produced to show that Walker was Governor throughout the siege, at first jointly with Baker and then jointly with Michelburne. There doesn't seem to be much doubt that after Baker's death, Michelburne continued as joint Governor with Walker in charge of military matters, while Walker continued to be in charge of stores and general administration. Michelburne lost his wife and seven children during the siege from the effects of the famine.

Exasperated by his failure to take Londonderry and by the refusal of the citizens to consider any of the extremely generous offers which had been made to them, Rosen decided to try terrorism.

On 30 June he sent a declaration to the commanders, officers, soldiers and inhabitants of Derry to the effect that if they did not surrender the town before 6 p.m. on 1 July, he would issue orders that all Protestants, protected or un-protected, from the barony of Inishowen and the seacoast as far as Charlemont, should be rounded up and herded under the walls of Londonderry. Those inside the town could either admit them for their protection (which would make further inroads into their now fast disappearing rations) or be forced to see them, many of them close friends and relatives, starved outside the walls and in grave danger from the cross-fire between the besieged and the besiegers. Failure to submit would also result in the whole countryside being destroyed, so that even if help came from England, the Protestants in the area would perish from lack of sustenance. Rosen also threatened that the houses and mills of the Protestants would be destroyed, and no hope of escaping would be left to any of them. He demanded that hostages and a full deputation with full powers to treat for surrender be sent to him before 1 July, failing which orders would be issued that when the town was finally reduced, no quarter would be given and neither sex nor age would be taken into consideration.

Rosen's threat caused great indignation among the garrison and people of Londonderry but the Governors and officers decided to ignore it. They sent an answer, signed by Walker and Michelburne, to the effect that according to this delegation Rosen had, or pretended to have, a higher command in the army than that of Hamilton and as Rosen threatened to break the protection already given to Protestants outside the city, they regarded this as indicating that they themselves could expect no mercy whatever promises might be made. They pointed out that Hamilton's commission bore the date of 1 May, 1689, since when a Parliament had sat in Dublin and had passed Acts forfeiting the lives and estates of Protestants. They therefore considered that Hamilton had no longer any power to treat with them either, until he got a new and fuller commission from King James.

Rosen then proceeded to put his plan into operation. He sent orders out to his commanders to gather all the Protestants living in the surrounding countryside, and all men, women and children who were related to those in Londonderry, and herd them under the walls of the city. The commanders were to provide them with no more food than the bare minimum they needed to sustain them during their journey. He had heard that a considerable number of Protestant 'rebels' from Londonderry, and large numbers of wives and children of men still serving in Londonderry, had retired for safety to the Belfast area. Accordingly he ordered a close search to be made there to discover anyone, regardless of age or sex, who was in any way related to the inhabitants of Londonderry, so that they too could be brought before the walls. His commanders were warned that they would have to answer to Rosen personally if they allowed any, even infants, to escape.

On 30 June, Rosen reported his intentions to King James and told him that he intended to exterminate all the Protestants in the area. He told the King that the Protestants had carried their obstinacy so far that they were now totally unworthy of King James's clemency and deserved to be starved to death, and he added that with the countryside around plundered and burnt, the English troops, when they landed, would find neither sustenance nor shelter, and accordingly must necessarily perish. Half fearing that King James might forbid him to carry out these plans, Rosen instructed his Irish dragoons to start carrying out his orders with the utmost vigour, without even waiting for the King's reply.

The first group of Protestant prisoners, men, women and children, about 200 in number, were driven under the walls on 2 July. When they first appeared the besieged, mistaking them for enemy forces, began to fire on them. Fortunately their aim was not good that morning, and they found out that these people were the first victims of Rosen's threatened plan before any of the Protestants had been injured in the firing.

On the following day, 3 July, more Protestants were driven in under the walls. Ash puts the number at 1,000; Walker says several thousand, while King says that some of the Irish officers admitted that they had rounded up as many as 7,000. And these were from an area of approximately ten miles around the city. Rosen's ultimate plan was to extend his collection of Protestant victims as far as Charlemont, Carrickfergus and Antrim.

Among the first parties were many young people and children, as well as pregnant women, some of whom died on the journey. They were herded together like animals and confined from time to time in dirty pounds — roofless enclosures normally used for quartering stray cattle. The cries of those who were driven in under the walls, before the drawn swords of the Irish soldiers, were very distressing to the besieged but also increased their determination to resist at all costs, since they now saw what sort of treatment they themselves could expect if they submitted. To their surprise, when at night they admitted some of the Protestants inside their lines at the Windmill, the Protestants urged them on no account to consider surrendering on their behalf.

As an answer to Rosen's action, the besieged erected a huge gallows on the Double Bastion, in full view of the enemy camp, and notified the Irish that they would start hanging all their Jacobite prisoners, one by one, if the Protestants were not immediately sent back to their homes. To add colour to the threat, the besieged also sent a message to the Irish army inviting them to send priests into the city to prepare the prisoners for death.

Twenty prisoners were next transferred from the private lodgings in which they had been housed, to the jail. When they heard what their fate was to be, they asked permission to send a letter to Hamilton. They were informed that they should write to Hamilton begging him to give the Protestants under the wall leave to return to their own homes and live peaceably as they had done since the beginning of the siege, in which case they, the prisoners, would be given the liberty they had hitherto enjoyed. Failing this, they could expect nothing but death.

A messenger then carried the following letter to the Irish camp addressed to Hamilton:

My Lord,
Upon the hard dealing the Protected (as well as other Protestants) have met withal in being sent under the walls, you have so incens'd the Governor and others of this Garrison, that we are all comdemn'd by a Court Martial to dye tomorrow, unless those poor people be withdrawn.

We have made application to Marshal General de Rosen; but having received no answer, we make it our request to you (as knowing you are a person that does not delight in shedding innocent Blood) that you will represent our condition to the Marshal General. The lives of 20 prisoners lye at stake and therefore require your diligence and care. We are willing to die (with our swords in our hands) for His Majesty but to suffer like Malefactors is hard, nor can we lay our Blood to the charge of the Garrison, and the rest having used and treated us with all Civility imaginable.

We remain,
Your most dutiful and dying Freinds, Netervill (Write by another hand! he himself has lost the fingers of his right hand)   E. Butler,   G. Aylmor, – MacDonnel, – Darcy, Etc., In the name of all the rest.

Hamilton's reply was brief and to the point:

Gentlemen,
In answer to yours; What those poor People are like to suffer, they may thank themselves for, being their own fault; which they may prevent by accepting the Conditions have been offer'd them; and if you suffer in this, it cannot be help'd, but we shall be revenged on many Thousands of those People (as well innocent as others) within or without that City.

James wrote on 3 July commanding Rosen not to put his plan into execution, but to send the men, women and children back to their homes without injuring them. As regards Rosen's plan to devastate the area around

Londonderry, he said: 'We approve of it as necessary to distress our enemies.' James added that he believed that Rosen's presence was necessary for the success of his army at Londonderry, and stated that it was his pleasure that Rosen should remain there until further orders. At the same time, he despatched couriers to all the commanders to whom Rosen had written, with messages commanding them to refuse obedience to Rosen's orders. Melfort remarked that if Rosen had been one of King James's subjects, he would have had him hanged. Avaux also refers to King James's exasperation that Rosen should issue such a command without reference to him, though Avaux himself didn't seem to disapprove of Rosen's actions in the matter. No more did Louis XIV, who later made him a Marshal of France.

At the same time Melfort wrote to Hamilton saying that the King was well satisfied with his proceedings and did not doubt that he would after all 'have the honour to finish the business of Derry with success and without employing any of these extraordinary means the King has expressly commanded to forbear'.

But in fact, the Protestants under the walls were allowed to go home – on 3 or 4 July – *before* Rosen had received James's order commanding him not to put his plan into effect. It is unlikely that Rosen was over-concerned about the fate of the twenty Jacobite prisoners who were under sentence of death. It is far more likely that he made this decision because he realized that his plan was simply not working. The Protestants were not, as Rosen had expected they would be, taken within the walls further to deplete the vanishing rations of the garrison, nor did they even seek to be allowed in. Some accounts have it that it was Hamilton who gave the order to allow the Protestants to go home, but even if this were so, Rosen as senior officer must have given his assent.

On 5 July, Rosen received James's letter and immediately replied that he thought he might have been able to induce the garrison of Londonderry to surrender by threatening them in this way, but that the threat had produced no effect. He told the King that he had not put his full plan into effect but had merely presented before the walls a small number of accomplices of the besieged to see whether this would make any impression on them, but, he added, 'they have the cruelty to fire on them, and refuse them every kind of assistance, for which reason I sent them back to their habitations, after having made them comprehend the difference between His Majesty's clemency and the cruel treatment of their own party'. He also promised once again to devastate the entire area around Londonderry if Hamilton should be forced to raise the siege.

The Protestants were given money and provisions for their journey home. As they left the walls, the besieged managed to smuggle out about 500 old and enfeebled inhabitants while retaining, as new recruits for the defence of the city, some of the younger, fresher men. When the last of the Protestants had moved away from the walls, then, and only then, did the garrison release their condemned prisoners and take down the gallows which had been set up on the Double Bastion.

The episode ended in yet another resounding victory for the defenders of Londonderry and an ignominious defeat for Rosen and Hamilton.

XII   *Famine and pestilence*

During all this time, the fleet lay at anchor near the mouth of Lough Foyle and Kirke made no further effort of any kind to relieve the city. Or so at least it seemed to the garrison who, having no communication with Kirke, could not guess what he was about.

Kirke had in fact heard about Rosen's plan to push the Protestants under the walls and had ordered some of his men to go ashore in boats to see what they could do. They landed above Whitecastle, where the Irish dragoons were quartered, plundered the place and brought off about forty Protestants who were sent to safety in Scotland. This action alarmed the Irish army, who imagined that a much larger force had been landed and sent three battalions of foot towards Culmore.

A Mr Hamilton, one of the Protestants who had been rescued by Kirke's expedition, saw Kirke on board the *Swallow* and described to him in detail what Rosen had done. Kirke later issued a proclamation addressed to the commander-in-chief of the Irish army, referring to his barbarity, 'unjustified either to soldiers or to Christians', and adding that 'all such cruelties would be retaliated on all Roman Catholics of whatever rank or condition', a curiously contradictory statement since indiscriminate revenge of this kind could hardly be regarded either as soldierly or as Christian. Kirke also sent Rosen a letter which he had received from King William and Queen Mary. It said that if the barbarous usage Rosen had committed against the poor Protestants by driving them under the walls or any such like were continued, the same usage would be employed against the Roman Catholics in England.

On the day when Rosen was driving the first of the Protestants under the walls, Kirke had held a council of war which was attended both by the fleet's captains and by the military field officers. This council discussed the advisability of causing a diversion by sending a force to the island of Inch in Lough Swilly. He felt that as this island lies, so to speak, right at Londonderry's back door, it would be a suitable base from which to mount an attack on Londonderry overland, from the bog side. The island was fertile and offered plentiful supplies of grain to sustain an army, and Kirke had been assured that once a force had established a base on the island, they would be joined by thousands of Protestants living in the area who were anxious to take up arms and assist in the relief of Londonderry. The council of war decided to establish such a base on Inch and on 7 July a first detachment of 600 men, commanded by Colonel Steurt and escorted by the frigate *Greyhound*, commanded by Captain Jacob Richards, sailed from Lough Foyle and arrived at Inch on 9 July. They anchored about a mile off Rathmullan. (See map on page 70.)

On 18 July, the Duke of Berwick with about 1,500 of King James's forces attacked this detachment at Rathmullan, but was driven back with the loss of about 240 men. Berwick afterwards explained his failure in this action by saying that it was not possible to dislodge an enemy supported by frigates which fired incessantly at his troops.

Kirke's forces next rounded up thousands of head of cattle from the surrounding countryside and took them to the island of Inch for provisions for the troops. Others of these cattle were sent round to the fleet in Lough Foyle. A supply of powder and ammunition was delivered to the garrison at Enniskillen, who sent a deputation to Kirke with a proposition to relieve Londonderry by marching overland. Kirke himself had arrived in Lough Swilly on 19 July and had gone ashore at Inch on 20 July. He returned to Lough Foyle having sent further arms and some officers, as advisers, to Enniskillen.

By 24 July, the island of Inch had been fortified and 16 pieces of cannon were in position. There were also ten guns on two ships, each of which carried a complement of 35 men. Inexplicably, Kirke now decided that the island would be untenable if the enemy brought cannon against it, and decided to make preparations for what he called 'a handsome retreat'. He proposed that only a very small detachment of men be left at Inch with some further men on the two ships anchored offshore. By this time some 1,200 Protestant people from the neighbourhood flocked to Inch, and Colonel Steurt felt that by weakening the garrison at Inch, they might well be exposing these Protestants to slaughter. He consulted Captain Richards who agreed that any substantial withdrawal of troops from Inch would put the Protestants there in grave danger and would almost certainly lead to the loss of the island.

A council of war was held on 22 July at which the field officers of every regiment quartered there agreed to ignore Kirke's instructions and stay on at Inch. This council informed Kirke that they had decided to stay on at Inch until he sent more positive directions and until after he had considered the council's arguments against deserting Inch island at this stage. This council pointed out that by retreating from Rathmullan on the mainland to the island, the Protestants had left the place open for the Irish to destroy it and murder the few remaining Protestants left there. If the 1,200 Protestants now on Inch were deserted by the army, they could expect the same fate.

This letter is dated 25 July. The forces at Inch continued to increase and strengthen their defences and reports reached them that the Irish troops, expecting a combined attack from the rear, from a force composed of men from Enniskillen and from Inch, were deserting in ever greater numbers.

In point of fact, no attempt was ever made on Londonderry from the rear, but the operations at Inch served several useful purposes. For one thing, the besiegers were deprived of this very fertile island from which, before the operations began, they had been drawing much of their forage. Secondly, Kirke's men had been living on board ship in extremely cramped conditions for over a month and were out of condition; the opportunities which the Inch operations gave them for exercise were thus highly beneficial. Then there was the fact that the presence there of a Williamite garrison had the effect of drawing from the surrounding countryside a considerable number of recruits to the Williamite cause. And finally, perhaps most important, the presence of Kirke's garrison on Inch island prevented the Irish army from making the concerted attack upon Enniskillen which they were contemplating. Rosen, fearing an attack on his rear from Inch, which might be joined by the Enniskillen men, decided instead to send Berwick to take up a position on the River Finn where he could prevent the Enniskillen men from getting through to join up with Kirke's forces at Inch.

Now at long last, and for the first time, effective communication between the fleet and the city was established. Intelligence was received in Londonderry in the middle of July; the messenger was a little boy who with great ingenuity managed to smuggle through two messages from Major-General Kirke at Inch, and the reply to one of them. When he was carrying back the reply to Kirke's second communication, he fell among the enemy and swallowed the letter, so that its contents are not known. The boy brought Kirke's first letter through the Irish camp tied up in his gaiter; it informed the garrison of Kirke's activities on Inch and the reasons for them. The reply was made up within a bladder, in the form of a suppository, and carried by the boy concealed in that way. This letter, signed by Walker and Michelburne, acknowledges Kirke's letter of 16 July, and informs him that the garrison and people of Londonderry have only enough victuals to keep alive until 24 July. It adds: ' . . . above 5,000 of our men are already dead for want of meat, and those that survive are so weak that they can scarce creep to the walls where many of them die every night at their post . . . We are offered very reasonable terms from the enemy which we still rejected in hopes of relief . . . God knows what will become of us for they vow not to spare age nor sex. A great many admire [wonder] how such a Fleet as yours could be so long before us and send no victuals, whereas the wind presented fair many times'. Walker and Michelburne also inform Kirke that the boom across the river was broken in several places.

According to some accounts, Kirke's reply to this was carried by the boy tied up in a cloth button, but Ash says there was no letter; the reply was delivered by word of mouth. It stated that officers had been sent from the fleet to Enniskillen to advise and organize the Enniskillen men, who would be down in four days to join the English forces at Inch to help raise the siege. The boy carried the reply to this communication in a fold of his breeches and swallowed it when he was captured by the Irish army.

During the three weeks that Kirke's forces were digging in at Inch, things had gone from bad to worse in the besieged city.

Following the message from the garrison questioning Hamilton's power to treat with them, Hamilton had asked James for a new commission and full authority to treat on the King's behalf. On 5 July James sent Hamilton this new commission and the authority he required, and the terms show how desperately James still wanted to gain possession of Londonderry. The commission was authorized and empowered Hamilton to treat for the surrender of Londonderry on whatever terms he saw fit and stated that the King would ratify these terms, notwithstanding any fault or treason by the garrison or their adherents. Hamilton was instructed to let the 'rebels' of Londonderry know that he had now received this new commission, and to inform them that if they did not yield to his proposals, they would be excluded for ever from King James's mercy. If they would agree to yield up the town, Hamilton was to promise them their lives, their fortunes, a royal pardon for all that was past and a guarantee of protection in the future, and he was to assure them that none would trouble them 'in their houses, estates, persons, religions or professions'.

Three days later James wrote again to Hamilton telling him that he had been informed that the 'rebels' of Londonderry had offered to surrender the town if they were allowed to go with all their arms and baggage to join the fleet at Culmore. James could not believe that any such offer had been made because he thought that if such an offer had been made, Hamilton would surely have accepted it; however, if it were true, he urged Hamilton to accept these terms. Avaux wrote to Louis telling him that there had indeed been such an offer but he believed it was designed purely to play for extra time during which the rebel garrison hoped that Kirke would succeed in relieving the city.

Hamilton now acted on the King's instructions. On 10 July, he had ten bombs fired into the town, some of them falling into the old church and again opening up ancient graves and disinterring corpses. But one of these bombs was a hollow shell containing an open letter addressed to the soldiers and inhabitants of the city of Londonderry. It said:

> The conditions offered by Lieutenant-General Hamilton are sincere. The power he hath of the king is real; be no longer imposed upon by such as tell you to the contrary; you cannot be ignorant of the king's clemency towards his subjects. Such of you as choose to serve the king shall be entertained without distinction in point of religion. You shall be restored to your estates and livings and have free liberty of religion, whatsoever it be. If you doubt the powers given to General Hamilton by the king, twenty of you may come and see it with freedom, under the king's hand and seal. Be not obstinate against your natural prince; expose yourselves no longer to the miseries you undergo, which will grow worse if you continue opinionate; for it will be too late to accept the offer now made when your condition is so low that you cannot resist the king's forces longer.

Hamilton sent this message, like the earlier one, in another hollow shell, because he still believed that the soldiers and inhabitants of Derry were not being fully informed of the surrender terms and were in effect being forced to hold out against their will by the Governors and officers. There is some evidence that he was right in this assumption; for in a reference to the earlier message which was sent into the town in this way Walker says: 'Copies also of these proposals were conveyed into the town by villains, who disperse them about the town, but all to no purpose;for they will not entertain the least thought of surrendering, and it would cost a man's life to speak of it, it was so much abhorred.'

As most of the ships now seemed to have disappeared from the lough, the garrison decided to play for more time. One of the stipulations in the earlier negotiations which had been carried on by Colonels Lance and Campbell had been that six commissioners should be chosen to represent each side in the matter of drawing up terms for a surrender treaty. The garrison now decided to appoint six commissioners and set out their terms. The commissioners chosen included the Rev. John Mackenzie, and they carried a commission, dated 12 July and signed by thirty-four names headed by Walker, Michelburne and Murray.

The proposed articles on behalf of the garrison were drawn up very carefully on 11 July. They stipulated among other things that all persons in the city who had taken up arms against King James in Ulster or Connaught, or who had aided or abetted them, were to be pardoned of all treasons and other offences against the King or any other person and restored to their estates to enjoy all their former rights, liberties and privileges; that all ecclesiastical persons of the Protestant religion within the two provinces were immediately to have possession of their churches, chapels, tithes and other dues, and all other Protestants were to have the free exercise of their religion; that all persons in Londonderry were to have liberty to go to England or Scotland, and those who wanted to remain in Ireland were to have a safe conduct to Dublin or any other part of Ireland; that those desiring to go by ship were to be given passages; that all persons pardoned were to have their goods and chattels restored and were not to be forced to take an oath to James or be compelled to enter his service; that officers and gentlemen pardoned were to be permitted to retain one servant each and continue to wear their swords; that the citizens and townspeople were also to be permitted to keep their swords and wear them; that the rabble of the 'mere Irish' or half-pike men were to be disarmed and care taken to see that they did not kill, rob or spoil or wander in the country; that all troops and companies in Londonderry which wished to do so were to be free to depart by land or water to Culmore, to join the shipping there, and that they were to be permitted to go with their arms, colours flying, drums beating, lighted matches and a suitable quantity of ammunition. These articles were to be confirmed by Act of

King William III

'The Glorious Defence of Londonderry', a tapestry commissioned by the Irish House of Lords in 1728 and executed in 1732 by John Van Beaver from designs by Johann van der Hagen. The tapestry shows King James and his officers about to start the siege. This view is taken from the east, the

Waterside, and the windmill can be seen to the left of the town. The medallions show personalities (Major Baker, the Captain of the *Dartmouth*, Dr Walker) and incidents (the breaking of the boom, the death of Pusignan) connected with the siege.

The breaking of the boom. *Above* A Victorian engraving showing the scene from the seaward side as the *Mountjoy* and the *Phoenix* make their way past the wreckage of the boom towards the city. *Below* 'The Relief of Derry', a print made from a painting in Belfast about a hundred years ago. It shows the ships in the far distance (1); a group of apprentice boys (2); Governor Walker (3); Colonel Murray (4); Captain Ash (5); Colonel Michelburne (6); and, very faint in the background (7), the tents of the Jacobite forces.

Parliament and passed by Parliament or by the King under the Great Seal of Ireland. They were to be complied with by 26 July, but before that date commissioners were to be appointed for the city and for each county in the two provinces with authority to see that these terms were carried out. Hostages were to be given by Hamilton to be kept on board the British ships in Lough Foyle, and by the garrison to be kept in the Irish camps at Strabane, Lifford or Raphoe. During the time the treaty was being ratified and until 26 July, there was to be a complete cessation of hostilities, provided that in the meantime no army came to relieve the city.

These articles are insanely intransigent, but perhaps they were deliberately made unacceptable in order to play for time, in the hope that the relief forces would have arrived by 26 July. It certainly must have been clear to the garrison that some of these terms would be quite unacceptable to Hamilton, despite his wide powers and despite King James's obvious anxiety to gain possession of the city at all costs. Some of them would, in fact, have been impossible to implement; for example, Hamilton could not possibly guarantee that the Irish 'rabble' would not kill, rob or spoil Protestants.

In the event, after lengthy discussions, and possibly for their own reasons – they may not have considered themselves bound by terms dictated by a rebel garrison and may not have had any intention of observing them – the Jacobite commissioners agreed in principle to all of these demands except three: they would not delay the time of surrender beyond noon on 15 July; they insisted that the Irish hostages be kept in Londonderry and not put on board Kirke's ships in Lough Foyle; and they would allow no arms to the private soldiers but only to the officers and gentlemen of the garrison. This was late on 13 July; with difficulty the commissioners representing Londonderry obtained until noon the next day to return with an answer from the garrison.

There is considerable confusion over events immediately following this conference. This was the period when Kirke was moving his troops into Inch island and fortifying it, and it seems that it was around this time that Walker received the first communication from Kirke, carried by the small boy mentioned above. In his reply, as we have seen, Walker mentioned the 'very reasonable terms' which they had been offered, and threatened, if that is the word, to surrender if Kirke did not send victuals within fourteen days. This letter was written on 12 July, after the articles stipulating 26 July as the surrender date, but before Walker knew that the Jacobite commissioners were insisting on the earlier surrender date of 15 July.

The Council met on 14 July and resolved that unless the Irish army agreed to give them until 26 July to surrender, and unless they agreed to the securing of the hostages on board the British ships, there would be no surrender. On the question of whether the soldiers were to be allowed to march out carrying their arms, the point was left for the commissioners to settle in further discussions.

The Londonderry commissioners then went back to the Irish camp and delivered the garrison's answer. The Jacobites refused to accede to these terms and the negotiations came to an end. Mackenzie points out that if they had been accepted, the siege would have ended at this point in time. Of this period Macaulay writes:

> By this time July was well advanced, and the state of the city was becoming hour by hour more frightful. The number of inhabitants had been thinned more by famine and disease than by the fire of the enemy. Yet that fire was sharper and more constant than ever. One of the gates was beaten in: one of the bastions was laid in ruins; but the breaches made by day were repaired every night with indefatigable activity. Every attack was still repelled. But the fighting men of the garrison were so much exhausted that they could scarcely keep their legs. Several of them, in the act of striking the enemy, fell down from mere weakness. A very small quantity of grain remained, and was doled out by mouthfuls. The stock of salted hides was considerable, and by gnawing at them the garrison appeased the rage of hunger. Dogs, fattened on the blood of the slain, who lay unburied around the town, were luxuries which few could afford to purchase. The price of a whelp's paw was five shillings and sixpence. Nine horses were still alive, but barely alive. They were so lean that little

meat was found on them.

Walker is more prosaic, and in a way, more chilling. At one point he simply lists the vanishing garrison as follows:

July 8th. The garrison is reduced to .... 5520 men.
July 13th. The garrison is reduced to .... 5313 men.
July 17th. The garrison is reduced to .... 5114 men.
July 22nd. The garrison is reduced to .... 4973 men.
July 25th. The garrison is reduced to .... 4892 men.

These figures refer, of course, to fighting men only; the casualties among the ordinary inhabitants of the city were even higher. Walker also includes a rather grisly shopping list:

Horse flesh sold for .... 1s 8d lb.
A quarter of a dog (fattened by eating the bodies of the slain Irish) .... 5s 6d lb.
A dog's head.. 2s 6d.
A cat .... 4s 6d.
A rat .... 1s.
A mouse .... 6d.

Around this period the people of Londonderry were dying so rapidly that there was not sufficient time for the survivors to perform the burial rites, and the rats which came out to feed on the unburied corpses were eagerly seized and devoured. Although Walker quotes prices in sterling, money was useless and the only really valuable currency was oatmeal; a small fish caught in the river, for example, could be bought only by several handfuls of oatmeal. Leprosy, fever and other diseases were very common and James II notes in his diary that when the older, feebler inhabitants of Londonderry were pushed out to intermingle with the Protestants whom Rosen had driven under the walls, they were soon picked out by their wan and lean countenances and by their nauseating smell. Some of those who came out of the city were so weak that they collapsed and fell down dead after taking a few paces.

Walker says: 'We were under so great necessity that we had nothing left unless we could prey upon one another: a certain fat gentleman conceived himself in great danger, and fancying several of the garrison lookt upon him with a greedy eye, thought fit to hide himself for three days. Our drink was nothing but water, which we paid very dear for, and could not get without great danger; we mixt in it ginger and aniseeds, of which we had a great plenty; our necessity of eating the composition of tallow and starch, did not only nourish and support us, but was an infallible cure for the looseness; and recovered a great many that were strangely reduced by that distemper, and preserved others from it.' Mackenzie confirms this item of medical information, referring to the disease as 'the flux'.

The Jacobite accounts of the siege of Londonderry represent the inhabitants of the city as being far better housed and equipped to withstand the siege than the besiegers were to conduct it, and certainly in the early stages of the siege this was so; before the enemy bombardment and the effects of famine and disease began to be felt, the citizens of Londonderry were far more comfortably situated than the raw troops living in trenches, in appalling weather, and without proper medical supplies or attention. Nevertheless, it must not be overlooked that the besieged, too, suffered great discomfort during the siege, and particularly towards the close of it. They suffered not only from a grave shortage of food and water, and the diseases attendant upon an inadequate and unbalanced diet, but also from lack of sleep and chronic over-crowding. C. D. Milligan puts it very succinctly:

> Those who remained within the walls when the siege began have been variously estimated to number between 20,000 and 30,000. Taking the lower figure as approximately correct, it means that a city, encompassed with ramparts about a mile in circumference, and built to accommodate at the most a few thousand people — in 1706 the population was 2,848, and a considerable number of these resided without the walls — was called upon to accommodate 20,000. It simply could not do so and Avaux, conjecturing why Cunningham's forces had not landed, says Londonderry was so overcrowded that people had to sleep in relays, sometimes in the streets, sometimes in the houses. When the city was being bombarded, many went to the walls or outside to the Windmill because they were in less danger there. For thousands there was no place to sleep, and as

the siege progressed, fuel was exhausted, and water became
more and more difficult to obtain, while much of that which
was available was muddy. The tribulations of the besieged
were intensified by the exceptionally inclement weather which
prevailed in the summer of 1689.

In such circumstances it is natural that there should be fits
of despair and discontent and that rumours should be rife
among the inhabitants. One such rumour had it that Walker,
who had charge of the provisions, had a secret store. Walker
had taken over control of the stores at the time when he
became joint Governor with Baker, and there seems to be
little doubt that he expected relief to come from England
long before it actually did; otherwise the rations issued to the
garrison and the citizens would not have been nearly as
generous as they were in the early stages of the siege. When
help eventually came, they were literally within three or four
days of the end of their stocks of food.

At the beginning of June, inhabitants were still being
issued with a week's rations at a time, but by mid-June
allocations were being made at intervals of less than a week,
and according to circumstances. When Hamilton's offer was
being considered, the stores were carefully checked to see
how long the city could hold out, and by that time, as we
have seen, the inhabitants were subsisting on horseflesh, dogs,
cats, rats, mice, tallow, starch and dried hides. They were also
venturing outside the city walls into the fields and parks
around Londonderry, at great danger to themselves, to look
for herbs and weeds that could be eaten to dull the pangs of
hunger.

But despite the desperate straits they had reached, the
garrison made every effort to maintain a strict discipline. As
July began, the officers were ordered to remain on call all
night in one of four different places: the colonels, majors and
captains at Governor Michelburne's house; the lieutenants at
Mr Buchanan's; the ensigns at the Bishop's house; and the
sergeants at Mr Stuart's. By this time, the soldiers were
regularly sleeping in their clothes because it was feared that a
strong attack was imminent. If the enemy attacked, the
officers were to repair immediately to their various
companies and post them as directed by the Governor and

field officers.

At 4 a.m. every day, according to Ash's Journal, two great guns were fired against the enemy. This was the signal for the officers and all those who had been sitting up all night to go to bed; at the same time the volunteers and other inhabitants who were not enlisted in the regular companies went out and manned the walls until 7 a.m. Michelburne's *Orders and directions for the better regulating of their Majesties' garrison at Londonderry* stipulates that at the firing of two guns from the Royal Bastion at daybreak, the burghers were to march with their arms to the walls to relieve the soldiers, and that they were to continue on guard until 8 a.m. Burghers failing to report were to be fined for two offences and turned out of the gates on their third failure to answer this dawn call. Officers failing to report without good cause were to be counted as disaffected, cashiered at the head of their regiments, and imprisoned for the remainder of the siege. These orders were posted up on the Market House, the city gates and the Windmill.

But the shortage of food was the principal preoccupation of the garrison and citizens at this period. On 24 July, when even all the dairy cattle inside the city had been slaughtered for food, the council decided to send a sally of 500 men out to drive in some cattle which had been grazing between the town and Pennyburn. This incident is known as 'the battle of the cows', and it was an affair in which the officers were sworn to secrecy until the job was done; one explanation for this is the possibility that the Governors and leading officers did not want the townsfolk to know that they were trying to secure additional supplies of food in order to continue the siege. The password on this occasion, incidentally, was 'Orange'. The men were divided into three parties and two of these parties so surprised an Irish regiment under Sir John Fitzgerald that his men fled in confusion. They couldn't believe that such a 'poor, hungry, starved people' would sally out, and in fact, didn't even have their match alight when the Londonderry forces arrived. Lieutenant-Colonel Sir John Fitzgerald was killed, as were other officers, and some officers and men were taken prisoner. Walker says that it was during this operation that some of the besieged were so weakened by hunger that they fell down themselves in the very act of striking the enemy. Nevertheless, they brought back with them a good supply of stores, arms and tools and the food they captured included some oatmeal and mutton.

By this time estimates of losses on both sides were becoming pretty wild, and it is probable that the besieged were deliberately deluding themselves in order to keep spirits high within the garrison. Ash, who took part in this battle of the cows, puts the enemy casualties at 60 killed and many more wounded. Walker says that 300 of the enemy, besides the officers, were killed. The besieged lost only three men but failed in the prime objectives of the expedition; for the Jacobite forces drove the cattle away as soon as they saw the Protestant army sally out.

The garrison then tried out one more ploy to get cattle for food. They had one cow left alive inside the city, an animal belonging to a Mr Gravet. This unfortunate beast was taken outside the walls, tied to a stake, smothered in tar, and set alight. The theory behind this extraordinary performance was that the beast's cries of agony would bring other cattle in the vicinity pounding up to its assistance; and the garrison would then capture these other cattle and convey them into the city. The plan, however, misfired badly, if one could put it that way, when the burning cow broke loose and bolted. It was shot by the besieged as it ran into the orchard, and its dying cries failed completely to attract the attention of other cattle peacefully grazing nearby. The net result of the operation was the loss of one cow.

Although the cry was still 'No Surrender!' things were now getting desperate. It is hard to say whether there was any cannibalism. Walker, a clergyman, has stated that the inhabitants swore to eat the Irish and then one another before they would surrender, but whether things ever got to this stage or not we shall never know.

There seems to have been an air of unreality, almost of euphoria, when things were at their worst. Walker, by no means the most sensitive of chroniclers, remarks on this. He notes that the spirit of the men was so great that they 'were often heard discourse confidently, and with some anger contend whether they should take their debentures in Ireland

or in France, when alas! they could not promise themselves
twelve hours life.'

Apart from the records of such historians as Walker,
Mackenzie and Ash, who lived in Londonderry throughout
the siege, there exist other accounts of life in the beleaguered
city at this period. C. D. Milligan quotes a contemporary
manuscript in the British Museum entitled *Personal
Sufferings in the Siege of Londonderry*:

> . . . the huge multitude within the walls were torn asunder
> and destroyed in every part of the town by the enemy's
> bombs. Death met them at every corner, and even water could
> not be obtained without hazard of life. Great numbers were
> swept away daily by bad food and ill-lodging, want of rest,
> stench and dismal sights, the noise of cannon, the cries of the
> sick and wounded, the continual fear of death or famine, or of
> falling into the enemy's hands, the daily loss of their nearest
> relations and friends before their eyes, whom they were not
> able to help, women unable to support their infants, and other
> miseries they were under but which could not be expressed. At
> length they died so fast that room could scarcely be found to
> inter them, even the back yards and gardens were filled with
> graves and some corpses were thrown into cellars. In some
> instances, whole families were wiped out, and others from
> many were brought to a very few who were in a most
> miserable condition.

Milligan also quotes from the diary of John Hunter of
Maghera, who served as a soldier throughout the siege:

> I could not get a drink of clean water and suffered heavily
> from thirst, and was so distressed with hunger that I could
> have eaten any vermin, but could not get it. Yea, there was
> nothing that was any kind of flesh or food that I would not
> have eaten, if I had it . . . Oh! none will believe but those who
> have found it by experience what some poor creatures suffered
> in that siege . . . I myself was so weak from hunger that I fell
> under my musket one morning as I was going to the walls; yet
> God gave me the strength to continue all night at my post
> there, and enabled me to act the part of a soldier as if I had
> been as strong as ever I was; yet my face was blackened with
> hunger. I was so hard put to it, by reason of the want of food,
> that I had scarcely any heart to speak or walk; and yet when
> the enemy was coming, as many a time they did, to storm the

walls, then I found my former strength returned to me. I am sure it was the Lord that kept the city and none else; for there were many of us that could hardly stand on our feet before the enemy attacked the walls who, when they were assaulting the out-trenches, ran against them most nimbly and with great courage . . .

In what is one of the best chapters in his very comprehensive book on the siege, Milligan also quotes from the famous sermon by the Rev. Seth Whittle, rector of Ballaghy, in the final extremity of the siege, just before the relief of the garrison – it was published in pamphlet form in 1690. The Rev. Whittle took his text from a passage in Jeremiah I, 18–19: 'For, behold, I have made thee this day a defenced city, and an iron pillar, and brazen walls against the Kings of Judah, against the princes thereof, against the priests thereof, and against the people of the land. And they shall fight against thee, but they shall not prevail against thee, for I am with thee, saith the Lord, to deliver thee.' He said:

We have been surrounded in this poor city for divers months, beleaguered by a multitude of merciless and implacable enemies, exposed to dangers, without ceasing or intermission; we have been deserted by those who came to our relief; tempted by parleys and specious terms of capitulation; undermined by treacherous contrivances among ourselves; exercised with all the varieties of terror and amazement; the small shot hath poured upon us like a shower of hail, the great guns, like thunder, have shaken our walls; and the bombs, like lightning have ruined our houses; we have seen death in all its horrible shapes, and we are every moment entertained with spectacles of misery and mortality; sickness and disease are entered within our gates; and pale famine is visible on every countenance . . . But let this be your comfort, though they shall fight against us, they shall not prevail against us. For the Lord is with us, the Lord is on our side, we will not fear what man can do to us. Let them trust in Princes and the boast of their horses, but we will put our trust in the Lord. Wherefore, my beloved, let me exhort you to be steadfast in your duty, to be importunate to God in your prayers, to cast your care upon Him, with lively hope and well-grounded faith, to rouse up your wonted courage, to arm yourselves with your accustomed resolutions, to fall upon the enemies of God and religion, the destroyers of your estates and country, the inhuman murderers of your friends and brethren. Proceed with a steady assurance of success and victory, for the Lord is with you and will deliver you.

The effect of this thunderous sermon was heightened when Seth Whittle gave his life soon after these words were spoken, and just before relief arrived in the city. Nine other clergymen were killed during the siege, out of a total of thirty.

The Rev. Seth Whittle's reference to 'treacherous contrivances among ourselves' seems to have been justified. One of the factors which the Jacobites could always count upon was that there would be dissidents among the inhabitants who would not want to continue to hold out. Hamilton's policy of granting wholesale protections to those who elected to desert the city had some method in it, though both Rosen and Avaux strongly opposed it. By doing so, Hamilton hoped to achieve two things: to gain intelligence as to what precisely was happening at any given moment behind Londonderry's walls, and to undermine the morale of those who were determined to fight on. Throughout the siege he was extremely successful in the first of these aims; from day to day the besiegers knew the exact state of affairs in the city. Whether he was quite so successful in his second aim is not so sure because it had been made an offence, punishable by death, even to discuss the possibility of surrendering and consequently not many people did so. Those who lost heart simply deserted.

When Lundy petitioned Parliament that he should not be tried in Londonderry, Walker urged that he should not in fact be tried anywhere in Ireland, not because he had so many enemies, but because 'there was a faction there for him.' Lundy undoubtedly encouraged many of the inhabitants to leave Londonderry, but he also left behind him an element whose 'doubts and fears and questionable loyalty,' as Milligan puts it, 'the besiegers repeatedly turned to their advantage.' Spies moving freely in and out of the city were encouraged to stir up strife. Undisciplined elements were a constant source of trouble to the authorities. There were the rumours that Governor Walker had a secret store of food hidden away which very nearly led to mutiny. There was the duel between Baker and Michelburne. There were the rumours that Walker had agreed to surrender the town to James and was to be highly preferred for this service. On 11 July, the day after the Irish army had sent the first dead bomb into the city with its message for the inhabitants, it is perhaps significant that some of the besieged panicked and refused to obey the Governor and officers.

In the entry for 23 July in his *Journal*, Ash reports:

> ... some turbulent persons got together to raise a meeting in the garrison; their contrivance was to secure the gunners in the first place, and to nail up their guns, then to beat drums; they did not question that they should have assistance enough to make terms for themselves, and to give up the garrison. This project was overheard and the chief contrivers were sent to Newgate. Since Friday last we have had a court martial every day ... to rectify and set right all misdemeanours in the garrison.

And there were other incidents which somehow don't tie in with the picture of a bold, resolute, united, defiant garrison standing shoulder to shoulder against a common enemy. When Adam Murray was lying dangerously ill after being wounded in one of the sallies, a Captain D. Ross, a member of the Court Martial, was sent to search the town for some saddles belonging to Sir Arthur Rawden that were missing. He insisted on searching Murray's house, whereupon Samuel Lindsay, one of Murray's horsemen, who felt that so stout a leader as Murray should have been above all suspicion, took his carbine and shot Ross through the heart.

Ash tells how several citizens went out, with orders, on 16 May to parley with the enemy, and says that the Governor ordered a cannon to be fired amongst them. He also says that on 25 July, some of the enemy came near the Windmill and invited the besieged to come out and parley with them. Two went out and were killed by the Irish.

And as we have seen, when the council of war was planning the cattle raid, all the officers involved were sworn to secrecy until the business was finished, presumably because the Governor and officers realized how the populace would feel if they knew that food was being taken in for the prolongation of the siege.

As late as 28 July, according to King James's own journal, 'the sergeants and soldiers of Derry sent out a signed paper to Major-General Buchanan, offering to surrender the town to General Hamilton on the morrow if they could but obtain some favourable conditions for themselves.' Avaux puts it differently. He says that 'six sergeants were come to offer on behalf of the garrison to surrender the place on the following day, and they would hand over the Governor, who was opposed to surrender.' Avaux comments that this may merely have been yet another ruse to gain more time, an explanation naturally enough eagerly seized upon by the Williamite writers to explain away what seems like an unseemly breach in the ranks of the faithful.

But having said all that, and allowing that there may have been some intimidation and that many who wanted to surrender were afraid to do so, it doesn't seem likely that the city could have held out for so long if a majority of the people, civilians and soldiers alike, were not determined to fight to the end for their civil and religious liberties. They had been promised help from England and one can imagine how the joy that arose in their hearts at the sight of the Fleet in Lough Foyle must have turned to bitter despair as week after week passed without any attempt to relieve the city. When, in July, the besieged took part in talks to negotiate a surrender, there were probably thousands in the city who, no matter what terms were offered, would have refused to have any dealings with the enemy. There were others who believed that although the surrender terms in all conscience were generous enough, once the city surrendered the Irish army would go back on its word and allow them no quarter. All Hamilton's efforts to weaken their resolve by granting protections on a large scale and by offering attractive surrender terms had not only failed to alter the resolution of those who ran the city, but they had also failed to drive a wedge between the Governors and officers on the one side, and the garrison and townspeople on the other.

And one fact cannot be denied: that over 8,000 of the inhabitants of Londonderry signed their resolution to defend their city in their own life's blood.

XIII   *The breaking of the boom*

After the failure of that final attempt to agree on terms for a treaty, there doesn't seem to have been much further communication between the besieged and the besiegers; but it is clear from Avaux's letters that the besiegers were now fully convinced that they were getting nowhere. 'It drags on,' he wrote, 'longer and longer. Affairs there are going backwards instead of forwards.'

On 19 July, M. Masse, a French engineer general, was killed by a cannon-ball as he went to lay a gun in a battery that he had constructed, and Avaux had already written to Louis to say that of the thirty-six French artillery experts who had been sent to advise on reducing the town, only five remained fit for duty. The remainder had been killed or were sick from the rigours of fighting in the field or trying to live in trenches and camps in the wretched Irish climate.

On 20 July, Hamilton had written to James to say that the besiegers now had only fourteen battalions, consisting at the most of 6,000 men, and that the besieged at this period were still about 5,000 strong in terms of fighting men. On the same day, James wrote to Hamilton to reiterate that it was of the utmost importance to His Majesty that Londonderry should be taken before any relief could be sent to the city, and that Hamilton was to use his utmost endeavours to see that this might soon be done. He said that he believed more men could be saved by attacking the city briskly than by prolonging the matter. If Hamilton and the other generals were convinced that the town could not be taken by force, then Hamilton was to continue the blockade for as long as it would be possible to do so with safety, every day being of importance because it seemed probable that the besieged had no provisions after 26 July – the date they had stipulated for surrender – and the winds were so uncertain that although there were forces in England ready to embark, they might yet come too late. James further instructed Hamilton that he was to cause the ruin of all the country around Londonderry straight away, lest if an invasion should come, he might not have sufficient time to do it. He was also to send the sick and wounded as far away from Londonderry as possible. 'And if, after all, as God forbid,' he concluded, 'you should be forced to leave a place that has cost us so many men and so much time, then you must guard the passage of the river on this side as well as can be . . . '

Hamilton called a council of war to discover the views of the other officers on this question of pressing forward with the siege. They were all agreed that it would be impossible for them to take the town with the forces at their disposal, except by means of famine. The general consensus of opinion was that the Irish army had been so reduced by sickness, fatigue and desertion, that there simply were not enough fighting men available fit for the task. A French officer called Girardin stated quite unequivocally that considering the forces which were before Londonderry, and those which were within the place, he was of the opinion that it would be impossible to take it at all, much less within a limited time. Hamilton himself thought that the most useful thing he could do would be to prevent or hinder the Enniskillen men from joining up with the troops from the ships that were still posted on the island of Inch and, as we have seen, Rosen had already sent Berwick to take up a position on the River Finn from which he could prevent the men from Enniskillen from getting through to join Kirke's men at Inch.

When James received these opinions, he decided to accept the advice of the council and sent new orders to Hamilton and Rosen instructing them to abandon the siege proper and concentrate on the blockade only for so long as they thought fit. Writing to Hamilton on 22 July, James ordered him to prepare to raise the siege, and then actually to raise it, unless Hamilton was of the opinion that by continuing with the blockade he could force the town to surrender for want of provisions, which by all appearances must happen very shortly since the besieged themselves had stipulated 26 July – presumably the last day for which they had supplies – as their surrender date. James also instructed Hamilton to blow up the fort of Culmore before leaving the area, and ordered Rosen to harass the enemy by laying waste all the land around Londonderry and Inishowen if he were forced to abandon it.

As the fourth week of July advanced, gloom and despondency descended on the Irish camp. Rosen would have nothing to do with raising the siege or blockade, stating that he had been against the whole idea of besieging the town from the start, but nobody would listen to him. This much at least was true. The remainder of the officers were primarily concerned about how they could best get away and cause as much devastation as possible before they cleared out.

No attempt had yet been made by the English forces to relieve the city either by land or by sea; and yet, for all practical purposes, the siege of Londonderry was now at an end.

If the besieged were alarmed and disappointed at the failure of Kirke's fleet to relieve the city, they were no more puzzled than the besiegers who had seen first Cunningham and then Richards sail into the lough with troops and supplies, and then depart again without making any serious effort to get either forces or provisions through to the hard-pressed city. At first the besiegers assumed that the delay was simply because reinforcements from England were hourly expected, and imagined that Kirke was waiting for them to arrive before starting operations, but when day after day passed without any reinforcements materializing, they began to suspect that there must be other reasons for the prolonged delay. This puzzlement shows up, among other places, in Avaux's despatches to Louis where he advances the possible explanation that Kirke was delaying any attempt to relieve the town until the last possible moment in order further to weaken King James's army and make the job simpler for himself; Avaux asserts more than once that whenever it became a matter of extreme urgency, it would not be really difficult to send in provisions by water. He had, apparently, very little faith in the boom constructed by his compatriot,

Pointis. That the boom was not so formidable an obstacle is indicated by the fact that more than once during the month of July it seems to have been broken by the effects of the tide and repaired again.

Around about the middle of July, for some reason Kirke seems to have shaken himself out of his lethargy, and resolved to take action. By now he had had Walker's message, carried by the little boy, to the effect that the garrison was on its last legs and that the boom had been broken by the tide. Richards records in his diary that the forces at Inch had received confirmation of this and had also heard that some of the great guns at Culmore and the river bank around the boom had been drawn off to batter the city into submission. Possibly this information emboldened Kirke to make his decision. At any rate, soon after the message from Walker reached him, and after he had received confirmation of this information from Inch, Kirke ordered three ships to be stocked up with provisions, went aboard the *Swallow* himself, and set sail for Lough Foyle. The three ships picked were the supply ships, the *Mountjoy* of Londonderry, commanded by Captain Michael or Micaiah Browning, a native of Londonderry; the *Phoenix* of Coleraine, commanded by Captain Andrew Douglas; and the *Jerusalem*.

Kirke arrived at the mouth of Lough Foyle on 22 July, and the following day sailed up the Lough sending the three supply ships – each carrying forty musketeers – ahead of him to anchor off Culmore and await a favourable wind for an attempt upon the boom.

Many historians have since asked, and attempted to answer, the question why, after so long a delay, Kirke suddenly changed his mind and decided to attempt to relieve Londonderry by water. If he believed that in addition to the boom across the river there were ships sunk in the channel – as there should have been – he does not appear to have received any information at this point that this was not the case. The news he received from Walker while at Inch was hardly sufficient in itself to explain so abrupt a change of tactics. However, Captain Rooke of the *Deptford*, in a letter from his ship dated 2 August, reports that when Kirke arrived at Inch he heard from the people of Londonderry that the enemy had withdrawn all their cannon from Culmore and the vicinity of the boom, and that the garrison were reduced to their last extremity and could defend themselves no longer – this could be a reference to the letter from Walker carried by the boy to Kirke – without a supply of provisions. Upon this, he says, Kirke immediately went on board the *Swallow* with three victuallers and wrote to him (Rooke) for a frigate to protect them in their going up which 'he did resolve that they should attempt at the first opportunity.'

A Parliamentary newsletter dated 2 August mentioned that 'positive orders' had been given to Kirke to hasten the relief of Londonderry. According to Macaulay, Kirke received a despatch from England containing 'positive orders' from Schomberg – who had been appointed overall commander of all the British forces in Ireland some time earlier in preparation for the proposed large-scale invasion – that Londonderry was to be relieved forthwith, and that accordingly he decided to make an attempt on the boom, which attempt, Macaulay comments, 'he might have made with at least an equally fair prospect of success six weeks earlier'.

According to Milligan, Kirke had already received an earlier communication from Schomberg, dated 29 June, with a postscript dated 3 July, in which Schomberg stated that His Majesty had commanded him to signify his pleasure to Kirke that as the council of war's only reasons for not attempting the relief of the city by water were the uncertainty as to whether the boom was broken or not, and the possibility that boats might have been sunk in the channel, then Kirke was to use all means to find out the facts by sending an intelligent person to view these places: 'and to get the best light they could of the matter, and to consult for that purpose the Sea Officers, whether it might not be possible to break the boom and pass with the ships, and that Kirke attempt the doing of it for the relief of the town.'

King William's further instructions at this stage were that if the passage were to be found altogether impossible, Kirke was to inform His Majesty what number of men, horse and foot, would be required to secure a position wherever he proposed that they should land, and that in the meantime

Kirke was to remain where he was and use his best endeavours to get a true information of the condition of the town, and what quantity of provisions of war or victuals might be wanted there, and he was to report on what might best be further done for the relief of the town, which was a matter of great consequence to the King.

Richards was at Inch when Kirke received this letter and his diary does not record whether in fact Kirke consulted the sea captains at this stage about the advisability of attempting to force a passage up the river. It is possible that this instruction from Schomberg, combined with the news from Londonderry that the boom had been broken by the tide and the heavy guns around it removed to batter the city, may have been sufficient to make Kirke decide to take action.

In *Londerias* – sometimes spelt *Londeriados*, a poetic narrative of the siege by Joseph Aicken published in Dublin in 1699 – the author suggests that it was David Cairnes who brought the express from King William commanding Kirke to relieve the town immediately. This could be pure poetic licence; for what could be more appropriate than that Cairnes, who had played such a key part in the early stages of the resistance, and who had undertaken more than one hazardous voyage in his own vessel to secure the relief of the city, should be the man who arrived with the order which set the seal upon its ultimate survival?

Apart from the *Dartmouth*, a frigate commanded by Captain John Leake, the only man-of-war immediately available to escort the supply ships was the *Swallow*, which drew too much water to go up the river. Captain Leake of the *Dartmouth* did however borrow the *Swallow's* longboat and crew to assist in cutting through the boom.

Having carefully considered in advance what had best be done, Leake conferred with Captain Micaiah Browning of the *Mountjoy* and Captain Andrew Douglas of the *Phoenix*, the commanders of the two supply ships which he had decided to escort into the city. The third supply ship which had been victualled at Kirke's instructions, the *Jerusalem*, was to follow them if they got through safely.

They readily agreed with Leake's proposal that he should go ahead, engage the guns at Culmore fort and any batteries still ranged around it, while the two supply ships slipped past him up river to the boom, which they would run against under full sail, in an effort to smash it. The *Swallow's* longboat, 'well-barricadoed' and manned by seamen armed with axes, would follow the supply ships and use the axes, if necessary, to help to break through the boom. The longboat would also be available to haul the supply ships up to Londonderry if the wind should fall light.

The plans for the attempt were completed by 28 July and evening was chosen as the best time for the assault on the boom. At 7 p.m. Captain Leake in the *Dartmouth* got under way and made for Culmore, followed by the *Mountjoy*, the *Phoenix* and the *Swallow's* longboat.

The crimson flag – Michelburne's bloody flag – was flying from the steeple of the cathedral to let the Fleet know of the city's continuing and increasing distress and, as Milligan says, 'to show them if not blowing hard, the wind was at least blowing fair, and that if they did not take this opportunity they might as well stay away forever.' In addition, eight shots were fired from the steeple to encourage the Fleet to hasten the relief.

The Fleet answered by firing off six guns as an intimation that an attempt would be made as soon as the tide turned. It was a Sunday evening, and Walker had just finished preaching a sermon in the cathedral, assuring the congregation yet again that God would at last deliver them.

About an hour after the sermon had ended, at sunset, a sentinel on the cathedral steeple saw three ships heading up the lough towards Culmore, and the garrison turned out and watched from the walls as the ships ran the gauntlet of the Jacobite guns. These had been brought back from the city to Culmore fort by the besiegers who, when they saw eleven ships in the lough, concluded that an attempt to relieve the city by sea must now be imminent.

In addition to Culmore, the Jacobites had two other forts on the same side of the river, one called Newfort, between the boom and Culmore Castle, and the other called Charlesfort, at the boom and extending on both sides of it, towards Londonderry on one side and towards Culmore fort on the other. On the right bank of the river there was yet another Jacobite stronghold called Grangefort. The Jacobite forces were ranged on both sides of the river to join the attack from the batteries as the relief ships attempted to smash the boom. The width of the river where the boom was erected was about 700 feet at low water and about 1,450 feet at high tide, and the Irish troops had placed about four guns and about 2,000 small shot all along the river at this point.

There was quite a stiff breeze blowing when the *Dartmouth* and *Mountjoy* got under way. The *Phoenix* had been instructed not to weigh anchor until the *Dartmouth* had engaged Culmore fort. The third supply ship, the *Jerusalem*, was to remain at anchor until a signal had been given from the *Dartmouth* indicating that the first two supply ships were safely past the boom. The *Swallow's* longboat was to accompany the *Mountjoy* to the boom.

When he reached Culmore, Captain Leake in the *Dartmouth* was fired upon with both large and small shot, but· held his own fire until the *Dartmouth* was in position between the shore batteries and the supply ships, when he began to batter the fort with his guns, so that the supply ships could pass by under the shelter of his fire. The *Dartmouth* finally came to anchor within a musket shot of the fort, and between it and the two supply ships. By now the wind had fallen very light, but the *Mountjoy* carried on towards the boom, accompanied by the *Swallow's* longboat.

Accounts of what actually happened at the boom vary a good deal, but it seems likely that the sailors in the longboat hacked away at the wooden part of the boom with their axes, while the ropes or chains were broken by sheer weight of the *Mountjoy* as she carried her way on to the boom. When the *Mountjoy* first struck the boom, she recoiled and ran aground, stern foremost, in the shallow water on the right bank of the river.

The engagement was being eagerly watched by the garrison from Londonderry's walls, but with all the smoke from the guns it was not easy to see exactly what was happening. When the smoke cleared, they could see the *Mountjoy* aground with the Irish troops swarming down the river banks to board her. The soldiers on board the *Mountjoy* and the crew held their fire and, it is said, allowed the Irish horse to come within a pike's length of the boat – this is probably an exaggeration – before firing on them from three cannon loaded with partridge shot which killed a number and put the remainder to flight. Even more important, the recoil effect from the cannon fire dislodged the *Mountjoy* from the river bank and the rising tide soon floated her clear. According to the Protestant legend the *Mountjoy* then crashed her way through the breach in the boom, and the *Phoenix*, which had also been engaging the batteries ashore, followed her to the boom and passed through the opening.

But the wind, according to all accounts, had by now fallen completely light, and the *Swallow*'s longboat had to tow the *Mountjoy* all the way up the river from the boom to the quay, so that the *Phoenix* actually arrived first. The *Mountjoy* was carrying the dead body of her commander, Captain Micaiah Browning, shot in the head as he stood on the deck with a drawn sword, encouraging his men in the thick of the battle.

According to Macaulay, the *Phoenix* in fact slipped through the breach in the boom while the *Mountjoy* was still fast in the mud. On the face of it this seems more likely, and it could be that the legend that the *Mountjoy* was first through the boom is part of the Protestant mythology which surrounds the whole affair; it would, after all, be only right and fitting that the *Mountjoy*, a Londonderry ship, with her Londonderry-born master lying dead on board, should be first through the boom, which in itself is yet another symbol. But if, in fact, the *Phoenix* did pass through first while the *Mountjoy* was still aground, this would explain how the *Phoenix* arrived first at Derry quay, *under sail*, while the *Mountjoy* had to be towed in later, after the wind fell away completely. If this is the truth, it reflects no discredit on her master, Micaiah Browning, whose widow was later decorated by King William; for his, after all, was the honour of breaking the boom.

While the *Mountjoy* and the *Phoenix* were passing through the boom and making their way up river, the *Dartmouth* was continuing to keep the enemy batteries busy at Culmore fort. Leake continued to fire his guns until he saw that both the *Phoenix* and the *Mountjoy* had reached the city quay safely. The losses sustained by the relief forces were, in the circumstances, extremely light. Apart from Captain Browning, four sailors on board the *Mountjoy* were killed, plus five or six soldiers and one lieutenant. In the longboat, Bo's'n Shelley was wounded by a splinter in the thigh as he worked to sever the boom. On the *Dartmouth*, only one soldier was killed and one wounded.

One reason why the relief forces' losses were so light seems to be that the fire from the Irish cannon was spectacularly inaccurate on this particular evening. This is explained by the anonymous author of the *Jacobite Narrative* as follows:

> It is not so easy to understand how the ship came to pass scot free by so many batteries and yet in four or five weeks before, three vessels attempting the same were repulsed. The King's soldiers answered that the gunners of the battery, some of them, were this morning [it was, in fact, evening] drunk with brandy which caused them to shoot at random. But still there remains the question whether these officers became inebriated without any evil design or whether they were made to drink of purpose and to render them incapable to perform their duty that day, and whether the English money aboard the Fleet in the pool was not working upon them for this effect during the time they lay there on the coast . . . those gunners lost Ireland through the neglect of their duty. Others make the excuse that their guns were small and so few and could not have been effective against the ships, which again raises the question that a barge or two should have been sunk in the channel, and this surely would have saved the Kingdom for no carelessness or treachery could then have taken place.

It was 10 p.m. before the ships reached the quay, and the whole population was out to welcome them. A screen, made of casks filled with earth, had been thrown up to protect the landing place from the Irish guns and the work of unloading began immediately. First, barrels containing 6,000 bushels of meal were rolled down the gang-planks. Then came cheeses, sides of beef, bacon, kegs of butter, sacks of peas and biscuits and casks of brandy. 'Not many hours before,' says Macaulay, 'half a pound of tallow and three quarters of a pound of hide had been weighed out with niggardly care to every fighting man. The ration which each now received was three pounds of flour, two pounds of beef and a pint of pease. It is easy to imagine with what tears grace was said over suppers that evening. There was little sleep on either side of the wall. The Irish guns continued to roar all night; and all night the bells of the rescued city made answer to the Irish guns with a peal of joyous defiance.' According to Walker, when the relief arrived they had only two days' supply of food left — a total of nine lean horses and a pint of meal per man.

The first news of what had been happening in Londonderry reached the forces at Inch between eight and nine in the evening, when they heard the firing of the great guns at Culmore and Londonderry, but it was not until the following morning that they knew for certain that the ships had reached the city safely. The information was brought to Inch by several people from the Irish camp who reported that the *Dartmouth* had battered down the whole of the upper part of the fort at Culmore, leaving no shelter for the men. The forces at Inch were greatly pleased at the news and celebrated it by firing off a twenty-one gun salute. Kirke, arriving at Inch the following morning, confirmed these reports and told the forces there how Leake 'had behaved with extraordinary conduct and courage.'

For three more days the Irish guns continued to pepper the city with shot of all sorts, but the siege was now finally over. Indeed, as we have seen above, it had effectively ended before the ships even arrived and no further effort was made to harass the citizens of Londonderry. Instead, the blockade was lifted, the cannon, ammunition and wounded sent away, and parties were sent out to devastate the surrounding countryside, according to King James's instructions. Also, officers were sent out to recruit regiments for what was now clearly going to be a full-scale war with the English army in Ireland.

The sporadic fire directed at the town continued until 31 July, when the besiegers set fire to the countryside immediately surrounding Londonderry, burned down their tents and moved off towards Lifford and Strabane with a strong rearguard of horse, in case the Protestants should come out from behind the walls to harry them. They needn't have bothered; the besieged had devoured all their horses save the final nine, and so had no cavalry with which to chase them, and the foot were in no condition to repair the omission.

The Irish army halted at Strabane where they learned that the men of Enniskillen had just made a sally out of the citadel and had routed MacCarthy's army of horse, foot and dragoons. This action caused such consternation, according to Milligan, that MacCarthy's troops left Strabane in so much of a hurry that they broke four of their great guns into pieces and threw twelve cartloads of arms into the river. Many of the sick were left behind. According to Avaux, writing to King Louis on 30 July, nobody knew how the 3,000 or so wounded who were lying at Strabane were going to be moved because there were not more than three carts in all to be had in the area.

By 4 August, a detachment had been ordered out of the regiments at Inch to march with Kirke on Londonderry and to make arrangements for quartering Kirke's regiments there. Kirke, accompanied by Colonel Steurt and other officers, was accorded an enthusiastic reception by the military and civic chiefs of the city. Walker and Michelburne offered him the keys of the city, and there was a procession through the town. Kirke left Richards behind in Londonderry to make arrangements for the garrison. By 7 August, Kirke had again returned to Londonderry with his three regiments which were quartered at the Windmill and forbidden to go into the city proper on account of the disease, probably typhus, there.

So ended this great siege, according to Macaulay the most memorable in the annals of the British Isles. The garrison had been reduced, in the end, from about 7,000 fighting men to about 3,000. So far as the citizens are concerned, it is hard to get accurate figures, but a letter from George Holmes, a Londonderry citizen, to a William Fleming, written in November 1689, says: ' . . . but I believe that there dyed 15,000 men, women and children, many of which dyed for meat.' The losses among the besiegers cannot be accurately ascertained. Walker estimates it at about 8,000 men. Of the thirty-six expert French gunners and engineers who were sent to superintend the cannonade, thirty-two had been killed or disabled.

All differences now forgotten, the citizens of Derry stood atop their battered walls, which they had defended and which had defended them for 105 days and nights, surveyed with triumph the smoking ruins which marked the recent sites of the camps and tents and huts of their enemies, and watched with deep satisfaction the disappearing lines of pikes and standards retreating along the left bank of the Foyle towards Strabane, secure in the knowledge that by their valour and determination they had saved their own tiny corner of the Kingdom from the Catholic Irish peasants and the Pope of Rome.

XIV   *Postscript*

It is perhaps not without some significance that the present disturbances in Ulster should have started in the city of Londonderry. But before considering these disturbances, it might be as well to look at events in Ireland in the immediate wake of the relief of the city.

It had been expected that Schomberg would reach Ireland while Londonderry was still under siege, but it was not until 13 August that he arrived in Belfast Lough with a mixed force of 10,000 Dutch, Huguenot and freshly-levied English forces. After a winter of minor skirmishes which settled nothing, Schomberg was joined the following summer by King William who landed at Carrickfergus with 15,000 troops, some of them from the army of the Netherlands. James, with between 25,000 and 30,000 men, confronted William – who had nearly 40,000 men and was far better equipped with artillery – at the River Boyne thirty miles north of Dublin towards the end of June.

The battle took place on 1 July. James was driven from his position with about 1,500 casualties (as against William's 400*) and his army retreated towards the River Shannon. James himself fled to Dublin and thence to France where his renewed appeals for a fresh army to retake his kingdom were ignored by Louis. One part of the Jacobite army then fell back on Limerick, while another section withdrew to Galway.

After a prolonged and bloody siege at Limerick, which was repulsed at the third break-through, and yet another siege at Athlone and a battle in Aughrim, Co. Galway – King William

---

*This total included Schomberg and the Rev. George Walker, the former Governor of Londonderry, then bishop-designate for the See of Derry.

himself had returned to England after the siege of Limerick — Patrick Sarsfield, the Irish general then commanding King James's troops, decided to sue for peace when the Williamite forces under a Dutch general named Ginkel laid siege to Limerick for the second time.

The Treaty of Limerick, signed in October 1691, guaranteed that Irish Catholics should enjoy such privileges in the exercise of their religion as were consistent with the laws of Ireland, or as they enjoyed in the reign of Charles II, a provision framed in terms so vague as to be quite worthless. Those Jacobites who were now prepared to swear allegiance to William were to have their confiscated property restored to them, and Irish soldiers who wished to enter the French service were to be guaranteed a pardon and a free passage to France.

In the event only the military clause was respected, though a number of estates were restored. But the principal result of the Treaty of Limerick was the emigration of 14,000 of Sarsfield's troops who joined what were known as the Wild Geese — Ireland's flock of exiled soldiers, serving as mercenaries all over the continent.

As for the civil provisions, once Ireland had been disarmed, these were conveniently repudiated. William, to be fair, did his best to see that the treaty was properly enforced, but he was not yet sufficiently sure of his own position to go against the will of the majority in England which at this juncture was violently anti-Catholic. A Dublin parliament of 1692 refused to ratify the terms of the treaty; and the London parliament withdrew from Catholics the right to sit in their own parliament in Dublin; laws were also passed decreeing that all religious orders should leave Ireland forthwith.

Then there followed a dark century during which a whole series of Penal Laws were imposed, ostensibly to punish the Irish for their support of King James, but in fact to limit their political power. These laws virtually removed all their rights as citizens. They could not vote, or hold military or civil posts, or become lawyers or teachers, or sit in parliament, or even own a horse worth more than five pounds. Bit by bit these laws were chipped away, but many of them remained in force for over a hundred years though in practice they could not possibly all be strictly enforced.

For the best part of this century there was no serious attempt at an armed insurrection, for the simple reason that after the Treaty of Limerick the Irish had no nucleus of an army on which to base a military revolt, but the whole period was marked by agrarian strife, as secret bands of armed men went around lynching land agents, burning out new settlers, killing sheep and tearing down fences. This agrarian warfare was particularly severe in Northern Ireland where Protestant gangs raided Catholic homes, ostensibly searching for arms, but more often with the idea of intimidating the Catholics into clearing out of Ulster. To defend themselves against such attacks, the Catholics formed their own private army, the Defenders, though inevitably, despite their title, some of their activities were offensive rather than purely defensive.

It was an encounter between two such rival gangs in September 1795 at the Diamond, Co. Armagh, which resulted in the formation of the Orange Order, a Masonic-style, semi-secret organization sworn to uphold the Protestant ascendancy. The Orange Order in time came to infiltrate every aspect of life in Ulster – it wasn't possible to get a job, or a house, or a seat in Stormont, the Ulster parliament, unless you were 'well in' with the Order – and it is probably no exaggeration to say that the Order was largely responsible for the existence of Northern Ireland as a separate state and for the way in which the Unionist party ran that state for fifty years. The Orange Order has lodges in Canada, the United States, Australia, New Zealand and even in darkest Africa, as well as in the United Kingdom; and they are all motivated, as the Derry Apprentice Boys Associations are, by one single impulse – a deep-rooted fear and mistrust of Catholics.

Every year the Orangemen march through the streets of the cities and towns in Northern Ireland, and indeed wherever they exist, to celebrate the victory of King Billy at the Boyne. But it is not a simple matter of celebration; the Orangemen themselves quite openly admit that. In the official history of the Order – *Orangeism: A New Historical Appreciation*, published by the Grand Lodge of Ireland in 1967 – the Rev. John Brown, one of the Order's official historians, puts it this way: 'On the twelfth of July and on other occasions he [the Orangeman] marched with his lodge behind its flags and drums and fifes, wearing his regalia . . . to show his strength in places where he thought it would do most good. Where you could "walk" you were dominant and the other things followed.'

Originally formed by Colonel Michelburne in 1714 to include those apprentice boys who had survived the siege, and others of their companions, the Londonderry Apprentice Boys Association first began the tradition of marching round the walls of Derry on the centenary anniversary of the relief of the city. The 'Boys' march around the walls of the city of Londonderry every year, pausing at the Bogside to throw pennies down into the Catholic quarter as a gesture of their continuing contempt.

Even Macaulay, who took a staunchly Protestant view of the whole business and never had much time for Catholics, had to admit that 'it is impossible for the moralist or the statesman to look with unmixed complacency on the solemnities with which Londonderry commemorates her deliverance, and on the honours which she pays to those who saved her. Unhappily the animosities of her brave champions have descended with their glory. The faults which are ordinarily found in dominant castes and dominant sects have not seldom shown themselves without disguise at her festivities; and even with the expressions of pious gratitude which have resounded from her pulpits have too often been mingled words of wrath and defiance.'

The century of the Penal Laws was followed – understandably – by a series of attempted rebellions, all abortive, and names like Wolfe Tone, Lord Edward Fitzgerald and Robert Emmet became part of the Republican mythology – they were, as it happens, all Protestants. In 1800, the Irish Parliament – which by this time had finally got rid of Poynings' Law – was abolished, and Ireland represented by a parliamentary party of 100 (later 105) members sitting at Westminster. A new generation of Irish patriots now fought for Irish freedom using constitutional means; a Catholic lawyer called Dan O'Connell won Catholic emancipation, and an Anglo-Irish landowner called Charles Stewart Parnell destroyed the power of the landlords by the first use of the boycott, and started on the long road towards Home Rule for Ireland.

After many vicissitudes, a Home Rule Bill finally went on the statute book just before the outbreak of the 1914–18 World War, but was shelved until after the war was over. The Orangemen of Ulster had already threatened that they would fight Britain if necessary to resist Home Rule and remain a part of the United Kingdom; and when, during the war, an impatient Republican minority in Dublin staged a rebellion which led to a guerrilla war of independence which led to a civil war, the Ulster Protestants felt grateful for the resolution of men like Sir Edward Carson, the Unionist leader, who had foreseen this possibility and had already laid the foundations for a border which would separate them for all time from the Republican Catholic Nationalists in the south. Unfortunately that border also isolated about half a million Catholic Nationalists – one-third of the total population of Northern Ireland – from their co-religionists and fellow-republicans in the south. No matter: the stout men who had kept King James kicking his heels outside the walls of Londonderry could easily handle a one-third minority of Papishes – and easily did, with the aid of the armed Ulster Constabulary and their auxiliaries, the B Specials, until a new spirit of civil liberty burst over the province in 1968 and blossomed under the harsh spotlight of world television coverage into a force that could no longer be surreptitiously 'contained'.

To be more precise, at the time of the formation of the Irish Free State about one-third of the people in the area partitioned off for the Ulstermen were Catholics. This situation was largely of the Ulster Unionists' own making; they didn't want the whole of the province of Ulster because it would have contained an unmanageably high proportion of Catholics, and they didn't want only the four over-whelmingly Protestant counties because they felt that this area was too small to be commercially viable, so what they settled for were the six counties of today's sub-state of

Northern Ireland, which include two with Catholic majorities, Fermanagh and Tyrone. But they felt that they could, with a two-thirds majority, keep the Catholics in their place and run the whole area, as Lord Brookeborough, a former Ulster premier, once put it, as 'a Protestant state for a Protestant people'. By now, Londonderry had become predominantly a Catholic city, but by ruthless gerrymandering the constituencies were arranged in such a way that the Catholics had little or no say in how things were run.

Ironically, it was the struggle for civil liberties for the Catholic people of Londonderry which led to the ultimate downfall of the Stormont regime and it was another siege of Londonderry, in 1969, sparked off by a parade of the Apprentice Boys, which led to the presence in Northern Ireland of the British troops.

'That day's parade', the *Sunday Times* Insight team wrote, 'was no more "provocative" than those of previous years. Indeed, it was a model of order and well-stewarded discipline. To discuss it in degrees of provocation, however, is to imply that it is like a students' demonstration in England – a basically pacific event which on occasion may be taken over by wild spirits. The point of the Apprentice Boys' march is that it is an annual political experiment of the most empirical kind. If the Catholics take the insult lying down, all is well. If they do not, then it is necessary to make them lie down. In August 1969, after nearly ten years of intense political excitement, the Bogsiders were not prepared to lie down.'

What happened was that a few Catholic hooligans started throwing marbles, stones and bottles at the tail of the Apprentice Boys' procession as it passed one of the entrances to the Bogside. The Bogsiders withdrew behind the barricades they had prepared and awaited the onslaught. The Royal Ulster Constabulary with, behind them, gangs of Protestant hooligans anxious to follow the police into the Bogside and teach the Catholics a lesson, penetrated the Catholic area and were showered with petrol bombs from the roof of a tall block of flats. The police withdrew, and like a parody of the original siege of Londonderry, the Bogsiders declared a 'free Derry', flying the forbidden Irish Republican tricolour and defending their 'No Go' area with sticks and stones and petrol bombs while the R.U.C. replied with C.S. gas, the first time it was ever used in the United Kingdom.

In the three-day siege which followed, six people were killed and eighty-seven injured. British troops were called in to assist the police in keeping order and the world knows what has been happening in the unhappy province since then.

* * *

It is interesting to speculate on what might have happened if King James's army had been a little less inept in their attempt to besiege Londonderry. If the city had fallen, Ireland might indeed have become a province of France, offering King Louis an inexhaustible supply of recruits, plus a number of good harbours closing off the western approaches to Britain. If that had happened, it is even possible that Napoleon might have been able to include Britain among his conquests and the whole pattern of history could have been altered. The British have far more reason to be grateful to the seventeenth-century citizens of Londonderry and their descendants than they appear to be. For it is one of the sad facts of life that nobody in modern England wants to know about the tiresome loyalty of the Ulster Protestants.

Thus, when the first civil rights marches in late 1968 and early 1969 turned into riots and the British press and television took the side of the Catholic 'traitor' minority, and the British troops when they arrived concentrated not on assisting the loyal garrison in putting the rebel element in its place but on defending those rebels from the Queen's embarrassingly faithful supporters, the Ulster Protestants were first bewildered and then infuriated by what seemed to them very shabby treatment of a people who had devoted their lives to upholding the 'imperial connection'. And when that resentment resulted, as it had to, in confrontations between soldiers of the Queen and loyal subjects of Her Majesty, fanatically determined to preserve that part of the United Kingdom, as they believed, on her behalf, and ultimately in the suspension of Stormont and the transfer of all responsibility for law and order to Westminster, the disillusionment of the Ulster loyalists was complete.

Whatever the outcome of the present situation, the Ulster Protestants will never recover from the shock they received when they discovered that their fierce loyalty to the Crown was regarded in the 'Mother Country' as merely tiresome, and their fidelity to the Protestant cause dismissed as an utter irrelevance in this day and age. And now, whatever happens – whether Ulster is ultimately integrated with Britain or abandoned to the Catholic Republican south – they know, most of them, that they will never again be permitted to run their part of the Kingdom as a tight little Protestant state. In these circumstances, it is possible that Londonderry and its legendary siege may acquire a new and even more alarming significance – or, more likely perhaps in the long term, may begin to lose its ancient and potent magic and become just another incident in history.

A note on source material

The first account which appeared in print of the siege of Londonderry was the diary published by the Rev. George Walker, who was Joint Governor of the city during a large part of the siege. Entitled *A True Account of the Siege of Londonderry* it was published in the autumn of 1689 and is full of gaps. Its publication was greeted by many complaints and protests and Walker was obliged to follow it up with a *Vindication of the True Account of the Siege of Derry* which was published in the same year.

The Rev. John Mackenzie, a non-Conformist, who was chaplain to one of the regiments in Londonderry during the siege, published his own account of the affair, *A Narrative of the Siege of Londonderry,* in 1690 to rectify, as the title page announces, all the mistakes and to supply all the omissions in Walker's account, and Mackenzie devotes a good deal of his space to undermining the role Walker played in the conduct of the siege, asserting that 'Governor Baker had been pilfered of several of his merited plumes, and Mr Walker adorned with them'. There is no doubt that Walker is inclined to blow his own trumpet loud and clear but it is likely that the reason for the animosity between Mackenzie and Walker is due to the fact that Walker was a Church of Ireland clergyman and consistently played down the contribution made by the non-Conformist ministers during the siege.

Captain Thomas Ash served in Londonderry during the siege but his journal did not appear until 1792, when it was published in Londonderry by his grand-daughter under the title *Extracts from a Circumstantial Journal of the Siege of Londonderry*. It is very brief, and like both Walker's and Mackenzie's, rarely mentions anything that was going on elsewhere in Ulster during the siege.

In 1794, Mr George Douglas edited and published a

collection of papers, poems and other odds and ends relating to the siege, under the general title *Derriana*. This includes a number of items of absorbing interest, notably a long but incomplete and probably highly inaccurate account of the siege in blank verse called *Londerias*. It was written by Joseph Aicken who was in Londonderry during the siege.

All of this material has since appeared in various editions — though not recently — and is available through the public library service or in such libraries as the British Museum Reading Room or the National Library of Ireland. It is worth noting that Walker's diary, Mackenzie's *Narrative*, Ash's *Journal,* and *Derriana,* along with a history of Londonderry, were all published together in a compendium volume edited by John Hempton and published by the editor in Londonderry and by Simpkin Marshall in London in 1861, under the title *The Siege and History of Londonderry*.

Captain Joseph Bennet, who was in Londonderry during the siege and was held prisoner for a time in the Irish camp, wrote his version of what happened. It was published anonymously by John Amery of London in 1689 under the title *A True and Impartial Account of the Most Material Passages in Ireland since December 1688, with a Particular Relation to the Forces of Londonderry*. Archbishop William King's *The State of the Protestants of Ireland under the late King James's Government,* which appeared in 1691, contains much useful information, as does *Ireland Preserv'd, or The Siege of Londonderry*, a tragi-comedy in two parts, each in five acts, written by Colonel John Michelburne, who was joint governor with the Rev. George Walker during the latter part of the siege, and published in London in 1705. Captain Francis Nevill's *Description of Londonderry as it was Closely Besieged by ye Irish Army in April 1689. A Description of the Towne and Workes About It. A Description of the Enemy's Camp*, has some valuable facts and an interesting map. There is a copy in the National Library of Ireland.

Lieutenant-General Percy Kirke's account of the relief of the city and various other actions in the campaign was published in Edinburgh in 1689 (*A True Account from Colonel Kirke of the Relieving of Londonderry*) but is not likely to be found outside the British Museum.

The most comprehensive contemporary account of the war from the Irish point of view is *A Jacobite Narrative of the War in Ireland, 1688–91*, edited by John T. Gilbert and published by Joseph Dollard in Dublin in 1892 in a very limited edition; there is a copy of it in the Irish Central Library. As mentioned in the text, although this *Narrative* was published anonymously, it is widely believed to be based on a manuscript dated 1711 originally entitled *A Light to the Blind* and written by Nicholas Plunkett, an eminent lawyer who was a zealous Catholic and an enemy of England.

For the French point of view, *Analecta Hibernica No 21*, published by the Dublin Stationery Office for the Irish Manuscripts Commission, contains much of the Franco-Irish correspondence between December 1688 and August 1691. It is edited by Lilian Tate and is published in the French of the period but is not difficult to read; it contains some fascinating insights into what the French thought about conditions in Ireland in the seventeenth century.

In 1824, the Rev. John Graham's *A History of the Siege of Londonderry and the Defence of Enniskillen* was published by William Curry of Dublin. Despite its sycophantic tone and its fanatically Protestant bias, it has some colourful details.

Far and away the most readable account of the siege remains that in Volume II of Macaulay's *England* (London: Longman Green, 1860). J. G. Simms has written a very brief but concise monograph *The Siege of Derry* with an excellent map of the city which was published in Dublin in 1966 by the A.P.C.K., but without any doubt the fullest account of the siege is Cecil Davis Milligan's *History of the Siege of Londonderry, 1689*, published in 1951 jointly by the Corporation of the City of Londonderry and H. R. Carter of Belfast as Londonderry's contribution, I understand, to the Festival of Britain. It is enormously detailed if somewhat *partis pris*, but above all, it is exhausively documented and is invaluable for anyone who wishes to pursue this matter further. Milligan has also written a fascinating two-part work, *The Walls of Derry*, published in Londonderry by the Sentinel Printing Works in 1948, which is a fund of historical and topographical information about the area and which contains some now valuable pictures of Londonderry before it was destroyed by the combined efforts of the property developers and terrorists.

On the subject of the Londonderry Plantation and the role of the Irish Society in developing the area, the definitive work is T. W. Moody's massive *The Londonderry Plantation, 1609–41*, published in Belfast in 1939 by William Mullan.

For the Jacobite point of view, apart from the contemporary Jacobite narrative mentioned above, J. G. Simms's *Jacobite Ireland 1685–91* (London: Routledge and Kegan Paul, 1969) is comprehensive and highly readable. Sir Charles Petrie's *The Jacobite Movement* (London: Eyre and Spottiswode, 1959) is also extremely readable, and Hilaire Belloc's *James the Second*, although grossly opinionated, is very useful and contains a number of quotations from King James's own journals.

For general historical background on Ireland as a whole, Edmund Curtis's *A History of Ireland* is accurate and comprehensive if slightly indigestible. Other general background books worth consulting include *The Story of Ireland* by Brian Inglis (London: Faber, 1956); *A Short History of Ireland* by J. C. Beckett (London: Hutchinson, 1952); or, for a briefer view, *A Popular History of Ireland* by Charles-M. Garnier (Cork: Mercier Press, 1961), a translation, incidentally, from the French.

Index